THE SECRET AUTISM ROADMAP

WHAT THEY DON'T WANT YOU TO KNOW

THE ALL-IN-ONE GUIDE WITH EVERYTHING YOU NEED TO KNOW FROM INITIAL DIAGNOSIS TO ADULTHOOD. REVEALING EXPERT STRATEGIES, TIPS AND TECHNIQUES TO HELP YOU GET THE BEST SERVICES AND SUPPORTS FOR YOUR FAMILY AND CHILD.

STEPHEN COOK

ISBN: 978-1-948750-24-0

The Secrets Autism Roadmap | What they don't want you to know!
Text and illustrations copyright © 2023 Stephen Cook

Table of Contents

This book is lovingly dedicated to
my wonderful wife, Ruth.

Her tireless efforts, unwavering support, and ingenious out-of-the-box thinking has been the driving force behind our ability to overcome the constant hurdles dropped in our path.

....

ACKNOWLEDGMENTS

Thankfully, so many great people have helped us out over the years that it would be challenging to include everyone's names, but we greatly apprecaiated all their help.

Gretchen, First Steps for Kids, Lisa, Roho Rossy, Luigi Lauri, Janine, Stephanie, Annie, Heather, Saol, CUSP, Stephanie, Eric, Doreece, Keyon, LAFEAT, West Side Regional Center, Soryl, Dr, Marian Sigman, Dr. Robin Morris, Lisa Popper, and Ramona

Bee Social Skills is dedicated to crafting the best resources to effectively tackle the challenges associated with Autism and social-emotional difficulties. We invite you to explore the comprehensive offerings at BeeSocialSkills.com, where you can also access free resources.

DISCLAIMER

This document is provided solely for educational and entertainment purposes. Every effort has been made to present accurate, up-to-date, reliable, and comprehensive information. However, no warranties of any kind, whether expressed or implied, are made. Readers acknowledge that the author is not engaged in rendering legal, financial, medical, or professional advice. The contents of this book have been sourced from various references. It is strongly recommended that readers consult with licensed professionals before attempting any techniques outlined in this book.

By reading this document, the reader agrees that the author bears no responsibility for any direct or indirect losses incurred as a result of the information contained herein. This includes but is not limited to, errors, omissions, or inaccuracies.

THE SECRET

The secret is the odds are against your success. It is challenging to be a parent of an autistic child. You are expected to be:

- **AUTISM SPECIALIST**
- **EDUCATIONAL SPECIALIST**
- **BEHAVIORAL EXPERT**
- **THERAPY SPECIALIST**
- **PROGRAM SPECIALIST**
- **EDUCATION SPECIALIST**
- **LEGAL EXPERT**
- **IEP EXPERT**

Somehow, on top of that, you are expected to understand how to maneuver through the constant bureaucratic hurdles that are dropped in your path as you attempt to get the essential services your child requires, but don't worry it can be done.

This book is a meticulously crafted to provide you with a significant advantage in their journey of raising a child with autism. By being able to recognize the challenges and uncertainties that come with parenting a child on the autism spectrum, and understanding the goals and objectives of each step along the way. You can develop a clear roadmap so you can approach your child's development with confidence and purpose.

Readers will find invaluable resourcse, with a wealth of strategies, tips, and resources that have been thoughtfully curated to empower you in maximizing each step of their child's growth. From early intervention techniques to navigating the complexities of special education law, the book covers all essential aspects of supporting a child with autism.

By arming yourself with knowledge and understanding, you will be better equipped to advocate for their child's needs effectively, making informed decisions that positively impact both their child and their entire family. With this book as their guide, parents can gain the advantage they need to foster their child's development, create a nurturing environment, and pave the way for a brighter future.

About the Author

Faced with the overwhelming complexities of the autism spectrum disorder and the lack of needed accessible information, Stephen and Ruth Cook embarked on a relentless quest to understand and meet the unique needs of their son.

His experiences as a parent led him to immerse himself in the world of autism advocacy, education, and research. Through perseverance and dedication, Stephen acquired extensive knowledge about various intervention methods, therapies, and legal rights for children with autism. This transformative process not only helped his child but also fueled his determination to assist other parents facing similar struggles.

Stephen's empathy, understanding, and advocacy skills earned him the trust and respect of many parents in similar situations. Realizing the hidden secrets and valuable insights he had uncovered, Stephen decided to share his expertise with the world. He felt a strong sense of duty to empower parents with the information they desperately needed but was often kept from them.

In this comprehensive guide, Stephen offers practical advice, essential resources, and personal anecdotes to help parents access the necessary services and supports for their children. The book covers a wide range of topics, including early intervention strategies, Individualized Education Programs (IEPs), navigating special education law, and tips for promoting social and emotional development.

Stephen aims to dismantle the barriers that hinder parents from accessing vital information and support systems for their children with autism. His mission is to empower parents to become confident advocates for their children, ensuring they receive the best possible care and opportunities to thrive.

Stephen Cook

THE SECRET AUTISM ROADMAP

Introduction

"Autism doesn't come with an instruction guide. It sometimes comes with a family who will never give up."

— Kerry Magro

THE SECRET

The secret is you have a hundred questions and aren't sure where or how to start. And a thousand more questions will come. At the same time, you are working through numerous emotions. You aren't sure what is happening, and you don't know who to ask the questions to or where to seek the information about recommendations and interventions you continuously need. All you know is making informed decisions that best suit your child's needs is essential.

By staying curious and inquisitive, you can better understand the most effective ways to support your child's development. This proactive approach allows you to actively participate in your child's care, enabling you to collaborate effectively with healthcare professionals, educators, and therapists to develop effective strategies.

Asking questions and seeking information empowers you to advocate for your child's best interests. You can make well-informed decisions, ask for modifications when needed, and ensure your child receives the most appropriate support.

This ongoing engagement in their child's care enables you to track progress, identify any changes or challenges, and make timely adjustments to optimize your child's growth and well-being. Parents are the best advocates in helping their child reach their full potential when they are well informed.

First Steps After a Diagnosis

This is a confusing time. You are going through the stages of grief, but it is crucial to start taking the first steps and looking for support and resources as your family begins this journey. Sometimes it will be challenging, but by following these steps, you are helping yourself, your family, and your child.

STEP 1
SEEK SUPPORT

You are not alone. It's essential to seek support from family, friends, and professionals. You should also join a support group for parents of children with autism.

STEP 2
EDUCATE YOURSELF

Learn as much as possible about autism and the resources available to help your child.

STEP 3
DEVELOP A TREATMENT PLAN

Work with your experts to develop a treatment and education plan that addresses your child's needs and teaches you how to handle behavioral issues.

STEP 4
LEARN HOW TO ADVOCATE

It is imperative to learn to advocate for services and resources. You will often need to work with organizations to ensure your child's needs are met.

STEP 5
TAKE CARE OF YOURSELF

Your health is essential. Caring for a child with autism can be challenging, so take care of yourself.

The Stages of Grief

Receiving a diagnosis of autism can be overwhelming and emotional for families. People will often go through the grieving process. That is a natural response to any significant life change. The grieving process includes a few steps but is not linear, and people may move back and forth between stages.

DENIAL

It can be challenging to accept the fact that a child has autism. This stage may involve feelings of shock, confusion, and denial.

ANGER

As reality sets in, people might get angry at themselves, their spouses, medical professionals, society, or even their children. Feelings of injustice, resentment, and unfairness may arise during this stage.

BARGAINING

People may seek alternative explanations, hope for a cure, or make deals with a higher power. This stage often involves searching for solutions.

DEPRESSION

Upon realizing the long-term implications, a person might feel overwhelmed by the challenges, the need for support, and the potential impact on the child's life.

ACCEPTANCE

This stage doesn't imply that all difficulties disappear; instead, individuals begin to adjust to the new reality. They acknowledge the diagnosis and focus on finding appropriate resources and strategies to help their loved one thrive.

What is Autism

Autism is a Spectrum of neurodevelopmental Disorders that have been combined under the umbrella of Autism Spectrum Disorders (ASD). The diagnosis criteria are the same for the entire spectrum, but individuals with autism may have unique symptoms, abilities, and challenges.

AUTISM SPECTRUM DISORDER

The most commonly used diagnosis for autism encompasses severe impairments to more mild or high-functioning presentations.

PERVASIVE DEVELOPMENTAL DISORDER (PDD-NOS)

This diagnosis was previously used to describe individuals who met some, but not all, of the criteria for autism. PDD-NOS is now considered part of the autism spectrum and is no longer a separate diagnosis.

ASPERGER'S SYNDROME

This diagnosis usually describes individuals with autism who have above-average cognitive abilities and relatively mild impairments in social interaction and communication.

CHILDHOOD DISINTEGRATIVE DISORDER (CDD)

This is a rare form of autism that affects children who develop normally for the first two years of life and then experience a regression in their development and the onset of severe autism symptoms.

Autism from a Child's Perspective

Gaining insights into autism from a child's perspective can be incredibly valuable in understanding their experiences, challenges, and strengths and developing strategies and interventions to meet their needs.

DIFFICULTY UNDERSTANDING SOCIAL CUES

Trouble understanding social cues makes it challenging to communicate and know when we are transitioning to another task, increasing anxiety and frustration levels.

HYPERSENSITY

SOUND: image a radio being played at full volume.

TEXTURE: clothing feels like they are made of scratchy wool.

SMELLS: certain smells can be intense and displeasurable.

TASTES: certain textures or tastes of food can be very unappealing.

HYPOSENSITIVE

The body craves sensory input such as swinging, spinning, and splashing in water.

Eye contact can be very overwhelming and uncomfortable.

They struggle with expressive and receptive language skills, making it challenging for them to initiate or respond to communication.

Sensory sensitivities can make motor planning and coordination difficult such as fine motor skills, which includes using utensils or writing with a pencil, or gross motor skills, such as running or jumping.

Gaining Perspective

To gain a child's perspective on autism, it is crucial to actively listen, observe, and engage with the child. This can involve seeking input from the child, engaging in play-based activities, and encouraging open communication with both verbal and nonverbal means.

UNDERSTANDING SENSORY NEEDS

Many of the things autistic children do are because their body is sensory seeking to help them feel better. Provide swings, spinning chairs, and chewing toys to meet their needs.

EMPATHY AND UNDERSTANDING

Recognize that your child is not intentionally behaving a certain way. They are dealing with their sensory, social, or communication difficulties meaningfully. Focus on the reason for their behavior.

SUPPORTING COMMUNICATION

Most likely, they are struggling with communication, so look for alternative communication (such as visual supports or social stories), which can facilitate their ability to express themselves.

MOVING FORWARD

Incorporate strengths and interests into their learning and therapy experiences. Reward them to encourage or enhance engagement and to keep them moving forward.

The Levels of the Autism Spectrum

The typical features of Autism are characterized by significant disabilities in interpersonal communication, social interactions, and patterns of unusual behavior. The features are then labeled as levels.

AUTISM SPECTRUM DISORDER

| LEVEL 1 | LEVEL 2 | LEVEL 3 |
| High-Functioning Autism | Autism | Severe Autism |

ASD LEVEL 1

HIGH-FUNCTIONING — REQUIRES SOME SUPPORT

- Difficulty initiating social interactions.
- Problems with planning and organization at times.

ASD LEVEL 2

REQUIRES SUBSTANTIAL SUPPORT

- Social interactions are limited to special interests.
- Frequent restrictive and repetitive behaviors.

ASD LEVEL 3

SEVERE AUTISM - REQUIRES SUBSTANTIAL SUPPORT

- Severe deficits in verbal and non-verbal communication.
- Narrow focus and becomes distressed with changing behaviors or focus.

Measuring Behaviors on the Spectrum

The "spectrum" also refers to the specific levels of symptoms, skills, or impairments that the person with ASD has. By looking at the spectrum this way you can more accurately develop interventions and supports to address problematic behaviors, and address skills or imparements to better prepare the child.

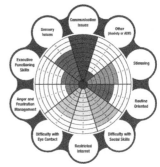

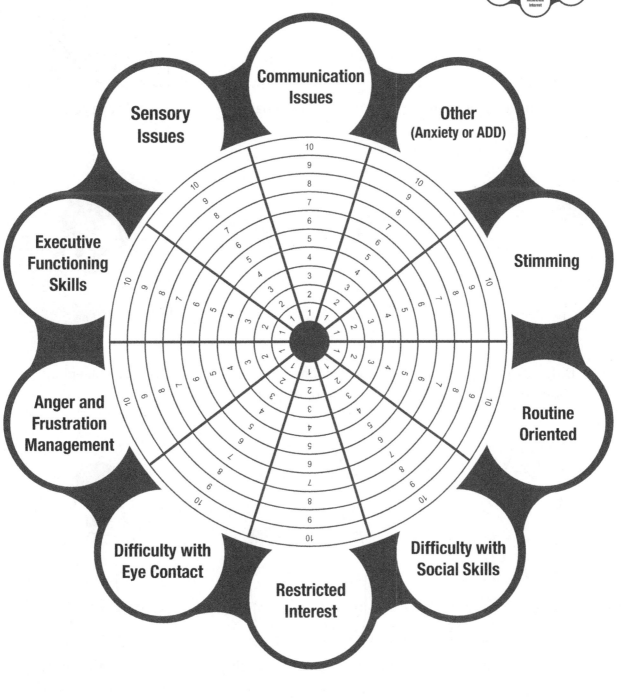

Recognizing the Signs of Autism

Delay in spoken language.

Insensitivity to pain.

Avoids eye contact.

Difficulty in playing
with other kids.

Lacks understanding
of fear or dangers.

Trouble sleeping.

Doesn't respond
when called.

Indicates needs by leading
adults by the hand.

Crying tantrums for
no apparent reason.

By recognizing the signs and symptoms of Autism, you can tailor their therapy approaches to address the specific needs of the individual.

Tiptoe walking.

Echoes words and phrases.

Lack of personal space.

Sensitivity to noise.

Resistance to change in routine or surroundings.

Fixation on specific objects or topics.

Sometimes doesn't like to be hugged or touched.

Enjoys spinning, lining up, and/or rotating objects.

Hand flapping, or rocking.

Understanding Autisitic Behaviors and Difficulties

Understanding autistic behaviors and difficulties is of paramount importance for parents of children with autism. It allows parents to know when and what therapies to provide their child to help them thrive. By recognizing and comprehending the unique challenges faced by their child, parents can tailor their parenting strategies and approaches to suit their child's needs. This understanding helps create a nurturing and positive home environment where the child feels understood, accepted, and loved, fostering a strong parent-child bond.

Secondly, understanding autistic behaviors and difficulties and being able to list them out provides the first steps to effectively advocating for their child. Whether navigating the educational system, accessing appropriate therapies, or communicating with other caregivers, being well-informed empowers parents to make informed decisions and ensure their child receives the best possible care and opportunities.

Additionally, it helps parents educate others, including extended family members, teachers, and friends, about autism, promoting greater acceptance and support for their child in the broader community. Parental understanding is pivotal in nurturing the child's strengths, addressing challenges, and laying the foundation for a fulfilling and successful life journey.

Becoming a Behavioral Detective

As you become familiar with being able to identify autistic behaviors you will want to understand why that behavior is being exhibited. The Behavioral ABCs help you understand why they happen by breaking them down. This allows you to understand what happens before and after the behavior. That will enable you to develop interventions to address the behavior.

Here's a breakdown of the Behavioral ABCs:

A ANTECEDENT

This refers to the events, situations, or stimuli that occur immediately before the behavior occurs. Antecedents can include environmental factors, social interactions, specific requests or demands, changes in routine, sensory stimuli, or internal states (e.g., hunger, fatigue). Recognizing the antecedents can help identify triggers for the behavior.

B BEHAVIOR

This refers to the specific behavior or response exhibited by the individual. It can include a wide range of actions, such as verbal outbursts, self-stimulatory behaviors, aggression, self-injury, elopement, or refusal to engage in an activity. Describing the behavior in objective terms is essential for accurate analysis.

C CONSEQUENCE

This refers to the events or consequences that follow the behavior. Consequences can be positive or negative and may influence the likelihood of the behavior occurring again in the future. Examples of consequences include attention from others, access to preferred items or activities, escape from a demand or aversive situation, or removal of an item or activity. Understanding the consequences helps determine the function or purpose of the behavior.

Communication Difficulties

Some of the most common communication difficulties experienced include:

DELAYED SPEECH AND LANGUAGE DEVELOPMENT
Delays in their ability to speak or develop language skills.

DIFFICULTY WITH SOCIAL COMMUNICATION
Struggles with nonverbal communication, such as making eye contact or interpreting facial expressions and understanding body language.

DIFFICULTY WITH CONVERSATION SKILLS
Struggles with turn-taking, initiating and maintaining conversations, organizing thoughts, and understanding social rules of communication.

A LITERAL INTERPRETATION OF LANGUAGE
Struggles with understanding idiomatic expressions or sarcasm, and may take language too literally.

LIMITED INTEREST IN COMMUNICATION
Narrow or repetitive interests and may struggle to engage in communication that does not relate to their interests.

DIFFICULTY WITH UNDERSTANDING GESTURES
Children with autism may struggle to use or understand gestures such as pointing, waving, or nodding.

Therapies to help with Communication Disorders.

- Applied Behavior Analysis (ABA)
- Speech Therapy
- Picture Exchange Communication System (PECS)

EXAMPLES OF DEFICITS IN COMMUNICATIONS

- **SPEECH AND LANGUAGE DELAYS**
  Difficulty with expressive language, or expressing their thoughts.
- **NONVERBAL COMMUNICATION CHALLENGES**
  Trouble understanding body language, and eye contact.
- **LITERAL UNDERSTANDING**
  Difficulty understanding sarcasm, irony, metaphors, or figurative language.
- **ECHOLALIA:**
  Repeating words or phrases they have heard.
- **DIFFICULTY WITH SOCIAL INTERACTION**
  Struggle with turn-taking conversations, and social cues.
- **LIMITED USE OF BODY LANGUAGE**
  Limited use of gestures.
- **DIFFICULTY WITH ABSTRACT LANGUAGE:**
  Concepts like time, and hypothetical scenario.

Executive Functioning Skills

Executive functioning refers to a set of cognitive processes that enable individuals to plan, initiate, organize, regulate, and monitor their behavior and thinking. Challenges with executive functioning can impact a person's ability to succeed in academic and social settings.

Here are some essential executive functioning skills:

- Planning and Organization
- Time Management
- Flexibility and Adaptability
- Problem-Solving and Decision-Making
- Impulse Control
- Working Memory
- Attention and Focus

With appropriate support and strategies, people can develop and strengthen their executive functioning skills, improving their overall functioning and independence.

Therapies that can help improve Executive Functioning Skills.

- Applied Behavior Analysis (ABA)
- Visual System

THEORY OF MIND
The theory of Mind involves recognizing that others have different thoughts, perspectives, and emotions than our own. Individuals with autism often experience challengesin Theory of Mind, impacting their social interactions and communication.

EXAMPLES OF EXECUTIVE FUNCTIONING SKILLS

IMPULSE CONTROL
- Calls out in class without raising a hand.
- Impulsive decisions.
- Responds inappropriately.
- Peers take advantage of them.

EMOTIONAL REGULATION
- Get overly emotional, and fixate on things.
- Cannot take criticism.

PLANNING
- Poor productivity.
- Cannot plan long term.
- Trouble choosing tasks that should be done first.

FLEXIBLE THINKING
- Panics with changes.
- Trouble understanding different points of view.

TIME MANAGEMENT
- Always late or early.
- Cannot manage tasks.

ORGANIZATION
- Trouble finding things.
- Loses belongings.
- Trouble managing thoughts.

Restricted Interests

Restricted interests are common and refer to an intense, highly focused interests that are often narrow in scope and may be pursued to the exclusion of other activities. These interests may be highly specialized and involve detailed knowledge about specific topics or objects.

While restricted interests can provide a sense of comfort and predictability for children, they can also interfere with socialization, play, and daily functioning. Therefore, it is important to provide opportunities for children with autism to engage in various activities and interests while respecting their preferences and strengths.

A great benefit of restricted interests is using them as rewards and incentives for children to reinforce positive behavior. They can help motivate a child to work towards a goal and can also help to build positive associations with the task or behavior being reinforced.

Therapies to help with Restricted Interests.

- Applied Behavior Analysis (ABA)
- Occupational Therapy
- Cognitive Behavioral Therapy (CBT)
- Social Skills Training:

EXAMPLES OF RESTRICTED INTERESTS

- Intense interest in specific subjects such as dinosaurs, trains, or particular animals.
- Fascination with technical systems.
- Music can be a strong interest.
- Excel in artistic mediums.
- Demonstrate a strong affinity for numbers or patterns.
- Video games can be a prominent restricted interest.
- Restricted interests in literature, language,
- or specific authors.
- May demonstrate a strong fascination with certain textures, sounds, or visual stimuli.

Social Skills

Social skills play a crucial role in the lives of children and can significantly impact their ability to interact, communicate, and form relationships with others. Developing social skills is essential to navigate social environments successfully. Here are some key components of social skills:

- Verbal communication skills involve expressing oneself through spoken language.

- Nonverbal communication involves using body language, facial expressions, and gestures.

- Active listening skills involve attentively and empathetically listening to others.

- Social cues are subtle signals and contextual information that convey meaning.

- Empathy is the ability to understand and share the feelings of others.

- Perspective-taking involves understanding and considering others' thoughts and beliefs.

- Social problem-solving skills involve identifying and resolving social conflicts.

- Social initiation skills involve initiating, and engaging, and maintaining social interactions with others.

Therapies to help with Social Skills.

- Applied Behavior Analysis (ABA)

- Social Skills Training

- Cognitive Behavioral Therapy (CBT)

- Play Therapy

- Relationship Development Intervention (RDI)

- Speech Therapy

EXAMPLES OF
DIFFICULTIES WITH SOCIAL SKILLS

- Limited facial affect.
- Delays in imaginative play.
- Delays in self-help skills.
- Not engaging in social play.
- Delays in speech development
- Inability to read non-verbal cues.
- Failure to understand the feelings of others.
- Difficulty understanding jokes, sarcasm, or teasing.
- Unable to carry a conversation.
- Repeats words and phrases over and over (echolalia).

Routine Oriented

Autistic children love routines. Routine-oriented behavior is often a coping mechanism for children struggling to predict events. A consistent routine provides a sense of predictability and control in their environment. It can help them feel more organized and reduce stress levels.

Routines are a powerful force in helping children deal with daily life. Routines, sameness, and even seemingly obsessive repetitive behaviors are a way to comfort themselves and to bring calm and self-regulation to an otherwise anxious mind.

It is standard for meltdowns when routines are broken. That is why teaching flexibility is essential. Visual schedules are a great way to provide a sense of routine to a changing schedule.

Being able to adjust to changes in schedules or prepare a child for a new event is essential to:

- Reduces anxiety
- Improves social skills
- Enhances independence

THERAPIES TO HELP WITH ROUTINE ORIENTED.

- Applied Behavior Analysis (ABA)
- Cognitive Behavioral Therapy (CBT)
- Visual Supports
- Social Stories

EXAMPLES OF
ROUTINE ORIENTED BEHAVIORS

- **DAILY SCHEDULE**
  Prefers to follow a set daily routine.

- **REPETITIVE BEHAVIORS**
  May engage in rituals or repetitive behaviors as part of their routine.

- **RESISTANCE TO CHANGE**
  Find it challenging to adapt to changes.

- **SPECIAL INTERESTS**
  Intense focus and adherence to specific interests or hobbies.

- **PREDICTABILITY IN ENVIRONMENT**
  Prefer a predictable and environment.

- **RESISTANCE TO SPONTANEITY**
  Will require advance notice and preparation for any changes.

Stimming

Stimming describes self-stimulatory behaviors that involve repetitive movements or sounds. It commonly refers to behaviors displayed by people with autism, such as flapping or rocking back and forth.

Many people use stimming as a coping mechanism to keep their sensory systems in balance. Repetitive movements, sounds, or fidgeting can help people with autism stay calm, relieve stress or block out uncomfortable sensory input.

IS STIMMING HARMFUL?

Most stims do not cause harm, but some stimming behaviors can cause self-injury and alarm others. If stims can potentially be harmful, that person may need help managing them. Some examples of potentially dangerous stimming are:

- Excessive self-rubbing or self-scratching
- Excessive nail-biting
- Head-banging
- Hand-biting
- Ear-clapping
- Slapping or hitting one

THERAPIES TO HELP WITH STIMMING.

- Applied Behavior Analysis (ABA)
- Sensory Integration Therapy
- Cognitive Behavioral Therapy (CBT)

**EXAMPLES OF
STIMMING**

- Hand-flapping
- Finger-flicking
- Rocking back and forth
- Pacing back and forth
- Spinning or twirling
- Repeating words or phrases (echolalia)
- Humming
- Hard blinking
- Opening and closing doors
- Flicking switches
- Finger-snapping
- Spinning or tapping objects
- Covering and uncovering ears

Sensory Issues

Sensory issues are commonly associated with autism. Sensory processing refers to how the brain receives, organizes, and responds to sensory information from the environment.

You can develop a plan to address sensory issues by creating an environment that reduces sensory overload. Then you can gradually introduce new stimuli in a controlled manner.

Here's how sensory issues can affect a person:

HYPERSENSITIVITY
An individual may have heightened sensitivity and intense reactions to sensory input.

HYPOSENSITIVITY
An individual may have reduced sensitivity or may seek out intense sensory experiences to feel sensations more intensely.

SENSORY INTEGRATION CHALLENGES
Difficulty integrating sensory input can impact a person's ability to navigate and make sense of the world.

THERAPIES TO HELP WITH SENSORY ISSUES.

- Occupational Therapy (OT)
- Sensory Integration Therapy
- Applied Behavioral Analysis (ABA)
- Cognitive Behavioral Therapy (CBT)

EXAMPLES OF
SENSORY ISSUES

- **TOUCH**
  Certain textures, clothing or physical contact is uncomfortable.

- **SOUND**
  Certain sounds can be unbearable, such as loud or sudden noises.

- **SIGHT**
  Sensitive to bright lights or certain visual patterns.

- **SMELL**
  Sensitive to certain smells or odors.

- **TASTE**
  Sensitive to certain tastes, flavors, or textures of food.

Difficulty with Eye Contact

There is no specific answer to why individuals with autism may have difficulty making eye contact. However, research suggests that avoiding eye contact may be due to differences in how the brain processes social information.

For example, eye contact is important in nonverbal communication and can convey emotions, intentions, and social cues. However, individuals with autism may have difficulty interpreting and responding to these cues, which can lead to avoidance of eye contact.

Furthermore, making eye contact can be overwhelming or uncomfortable for some individuals with autism, as it may require a lot of mental effort or feel intrusive. Others may prefer to focus on other aspects of their environment, such as objects or activities, rather than people.

THERAPIES THAT CAN HELP IMPROVE DIFFICULTY WITH EYE CONTACT.

- Applied Behavior Analysis (ABA)
- Social Skills Training
- Occupational Therapy

EXAMPLES OF
DIFFICULTIES WITH EYE CONTACT

- Avoiding eye contact
- Sensory sensitivity
- Difficulty interpreting social cues
- Distracted by details
- Communication challenges

Frustration Managerment

Managing frustration is an essential skill that includes regulating emotions and coping with difficult situations. Here are some common problems and strategies that can help with frustration management:

- **COMMUNICATION AND SELF-ADVOCACY**
  Encouraging them to express their feelings through communication can help manage frustrations.

- **EMOTIONAL REGULATION TECHNIQUES**
  Practicing specific strategies to regulate emotions can be beneficial.

- **SOCIAL SKILLS TRAINING**
  A person can help cope with frustrating situations by developing and improving social skills.

- **PREDICTABILITY AND ROUTINE**
  Creating a structured, predictable environment with visual schedules and social stories can help reduce frustration.

- **SENSORY REGULATION**
  Identifying sensory triggers and creating sensory-friendly environments can help manage frustration.

- **BEHAVIORAL MANAGEMENT, INCLUDING REWARDS**
  Rewarding positive behaviors and coping strategies can motivate individuals.

THERAPIES THAT CAN HELP IMPROVE ANGER AND FRUSTRATION MANAGEMENT.

- Applied Behavior Analysis (ABA)

- Cognitive Behavioral Therapy (CBT)

- Social Skills Training

- Art Therapy

EXAMPLES OF
FRUSTRATION MANAGEMENT

- Meltdowns
- Self-Injurious Behavior
- Rigidity Or Inflexible Thinking
- Task Or Social Avoidance
- Verbal Outbursts

Other

In addition to these core challenges, children with autism may also experience other issues that can impair their daily functioning. In some cases that may include ADHD or anxiety. When an autistic person also has co-occurring ADHD or anxiety, it can be important to take a comprehensive approach to treatment.

ADHD is a neurodevelopmental disorder that typically begins in childhood but can persist into adulthood. It is characterized by persistent patterns of inattention, hyperactivity, and impulsivity that can significantly impact an individual's functioning and well-being.

Anxiety is a broad term that encompasses various disorders characterized by excessive and persistent fear, worry, or unease. Anxiety disorders can significantly impact daily functioning and well-being.

THERAPIES OR MEDICATIONS THAT CAN HELP IMPROVE ADHD OR ANXIETY.

- Medication
- Applied Behavioral Analysis (ABA)
- Cognitive Behavioral Therapy (CBT)
- Social Skills Training
- Mindfulness and Relaxation Techniques

EXAMPLES OF
ADHD

- **INATTENTION**
  Difficulty sustaining attention and focus.

- **HYPERACTIVITY**
  Excessive levels of physical restlessness.

- **IMPULSIVITY**
  Acting without thinking.

EXAMPLES OF
ANXIETY

- **GENERAL ANXIETY**
  Excessive worry and fear about aspects of life.

- **SPECIFICANXIETY**
  Excessive worry about a specific aspect. Can be Social Anxiety, Text Anxiety, Health Anxiety or Separation Anxiety.

- **PANIC ATTACKS**
  Intense episodes of fear.

- **SPECIFIC PHOBIAS**
  Intense fear and avoidance of specific items.

- **OBSESSIVE-COMPULSIVE DISORDER (OCD)**
  Repetitive behaviors.

- **PERFORMANCE ANXIETY**
  Fear of performing in front of others.

What is Neurodiversity?

Neurodiversity is a concept that recognizes and celebrates the natural variation in human neurological and cognitive functioning. It emphasizes the idea that neurological differences, such as Autism, ADHD, dyslexia, and other developmental conditions are simply natural variations of the human brain rather than defects or disorders that need to be fixed or cured.

The infinity symbol is often used to represent the idea of infinite diversity and the infinite possibilities that come with embracing and accepting neurological differences.

The neurodiversity movement advocates for:

- Accepting and respecting neurodivergent individuals and accommodating individuals regardless of the intensity of their neurological differences.

- Challenges the medical model of disability, which pathologizes and focuses on "fixing" or eliminating differences.

- Encourages individuals with neurological differences to advocate for themselves and have control over their lives.

- Acknowledges the unique strengths and perspectives that neurodivergent individuals bring to society, such as the diverse ways of thinking that can lead to innovation and creativity.

- Emphasizes the need for inclusive education and appropriate support systems that respect and accommodate the needs of neurodivergent individuals.

The many concerns with Neurodiversity.

Overall the neurodiversity movement focuses on high-functioning individuals who can contribute to society in meaningful ways. Still, many people face significant challenges in their daily lives, and addressing those behaviors with intensive behavioral therapy appears to be stigmatized by the Neurodiversity movement. Here are some additional problems with the concept of Neurodiversity:

- Many problematic behaviors, specifically safety or self-injurious behaviors, require intervention and "fixing."

- Many behaviors related to frustration management are too extreme to accept as a unique strength and accept and accommodate.

The Stigma of Autism

Autism involves many behaviors that society finds to be frightening or uncomfortable. Some people with Autism may hit, yell, or hurt themselves. They may violate other people's personal space, ignore social rules, laugh, or make noise at the wrong time. These behaviors often result in negative attitudes towards those with Autism and their families and can lead to social isolation. Unsurprisingly, some families would rather avoid getting a diagnosis of Autism or isolate themselves at times to avoid the stigma of Autism.

Avoiding the diagnosis of Autism to avoid the stigma is counter productive. Early intervention and learning how to deal with problematic behaviors can help remove the stigma. There are many effective interventions and therapies available to help children with autism develop and succeed.

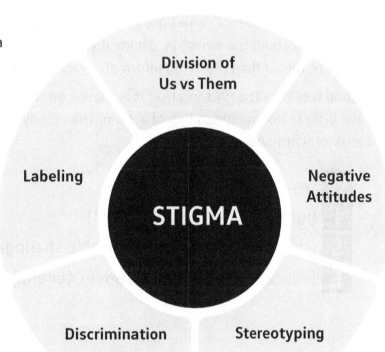

32%
OF PEOPLE WERE EXCLUDED FROM SOCIAL EVENTS

40%
OF PEOPLE ISOLATE THEMSELVES FROM FRIENDS AND FAMILY

BEHAVIORAL CONCERNS

A recent study found the more problematic behaviors a child had, the more isolated and excluded the family felt from friends, relatives, and social activities. The study said about 32 percent of the families were excluded from social events, and 40 percent isolated themselves from friends and family.

Dealing with Negative Interactions with Strangers

Children with autism and their families often find themselves in uncomfortable situations during encounters with strangers. Despite widespread awareness about autism, strangers can be outright rude, insensitive, or simply ill informed. A normal reaction for a parent is to step in and defend their child. These psychologically demanding public encounters with strangers are confusing, hurtful, and stressful for parents and children. Your job is to effectively judge if the comment being made is in fact 'rude' or comes out of an innocent ignorance and then, given all the information about the situation, decide if you are better off just ignoring a rude comment rather than providing information about your child's behavior

A good tool is called "W.I.S.E. Up!" it is "based on the premise that lots of people have little to no understanding of autism. The acronym W.I.S.E. stands for the four behavioral options:

W (walk away)

I (ignore or change the subject)

S (share what you are comfortable sharing)

E (educate them about autism in general)

You Own the Label

When to reveal an autism diagnosis is up to you. You do not have to use it as an excuse for an inappropriate behavior and you do not have to explain autism to everyone that you come in contact with. Having an autism dianosis can open doors and provide services you might not be able to obtain, but just like any medical condition you are not obligated to explain your child's diagnosis to anyone.

Evaluate each situation and decide what is appropriate. There have been many times when something has happened I just explained my son has a communication disorder. For for many sports or activities I would participate as an assistance couch, or we would provide an aide that would help out. In some activities such as skiing, surfing, and horseback riding we have talked to the company and brought in a trianer that had experience with autism.

Autism the Invisible Disability

Autism is often referred to as the "invisible disability" because many individuals with autism may not have any obvious physical traits or visible signs of their condition. Autism is a neurodevelopmental disorder that affects social communication and interaction, and exhibitis many behaviors associated with sensory processing. Although Autism has visible behaviors these are not always apparent to others.

While some individuals with autism may have visible signs, such as repetitive behaviors or sensory sensitivities, others may present as shy, introverted, or withdrawn, which can be mistaken for social awkwardness. Additionally, some individuals with autism may have above-average intelligence or academic abilities, which can further mask their struggles.

It is important to note that just because autism may not be immediately visible, it does not mean that individuals with autism do not face significant challenges and require support and understanding. Understanding and recognizing the "invisible" aspects of autism is crucial for creating a more inclusive and accepting society.

93% of people with disabilities don't use a wheelchair.

THE SECRET AUTISM ROADMAP

Autism History

"If you've met one individual with autism, you've met one individual with autism."

— Stephen Shore

THE SECRET

The secret is there is an epidemic of Autism. The term "epidemic" is not typically used to describe Autism. Yes, the prevalence of Autism has increased in recent years, but the C.D.C. says it is largely due to changes in diagnostic criteria, increased awareness, and improved diagnostic methods. Although an extensive study by the M.I.N.D. Institute Study in 2002, which did an extensive study, concluded the increase in Autism rates was NOT due to changes in diagnostic criteria, increased awareness, or improved diagnostic methods.*

The M.I.N.D. Institute Study summary states. "The unprecedented increase in Autism in California is real and cannot be explained away by artificial factors, such as misclassification and criteria changes, according to the results of a large statewide epidemiological study. "Speculation about the increase in Autism in California has led some to try to explain it away as a statistical issue or with other factors that artificially inflated the numbers," said UC Davis pediatric epidemiologist Robert S. Byrd, the principal investigator on the study. "Instead, we found that Autism is rising in the state, and we still do not know why. The results of this study are, without a doubt, sobering."

Needless to say in the end autism is not called an epidemic in the traditional sense, but it is considered a significant public health concern that affects millions of people.

AUTISM AFFECTS AN ESTIMATED

1 IN 36

IN THE UNITED STATES

*University Of California, Davis - Medical Center. "M.I.N.D. Institute Study Confirms Autism Increase." ScienceDaily. ScienceDaily, 18 October 2002. <www.sciencedaily.com/releases/2002/10/021018081039.htm>.

Increase in Autism Rates

The prevalence of autism in the
United States has increased
by over 1000% since 1970

Center for Disease Control (CDC) data

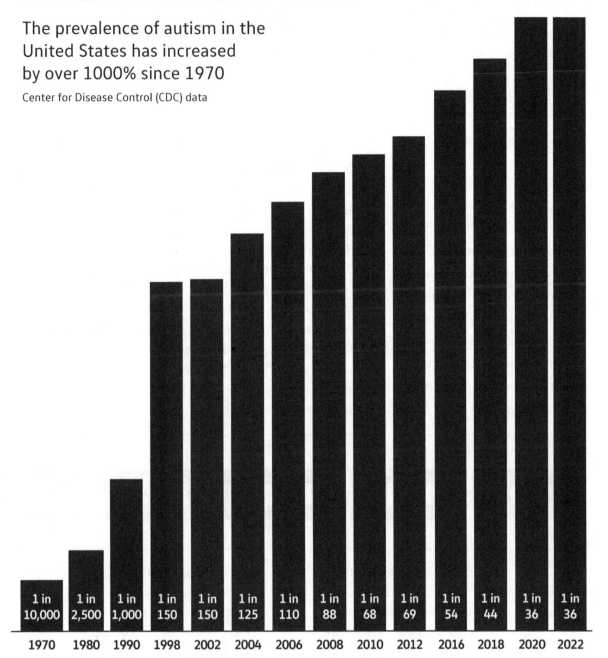

1 in 10,000	1 in 2,500	1 in 1,000	1 in 150	1 in 150	1 in 125	1 in 110	1 in 88	1 in 68	1 in 69	1 in 54	1 in 44	1 in 36	1 in 36
1970	1980	1990	1998	2002	2004	2006	2008	2010	2012	2016	2018	2020	2022

2022 AUTISM RATES IN CALIFORNIA
1 IN 22

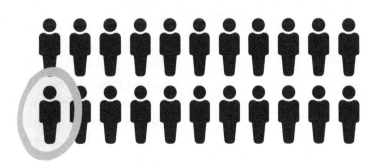

The History of Autism

Autism started being clasified in the early 20th century, but there are descriptions of people who were likely autistic that go back at least as far as the 13th century.

In the late 1700s, Jean Marc Gaspard Itard worked with a boy who had grown up alone in the woods. The boy was unable to speak or understand language. Itard felt the boy's behavior resulted from his deprived environment and worked with him on language and social skills.

Dr. Leo Kanner identified Autism as a social and emotional disorder based on a study of 11 children. He called it "Autistic Disturbances of Affective Contact" described it as inaction to the outside world with extreme autistic aloneness. There were similar patterns in social skill deficits, abnormal language development, and insistence on sameness.

Elwyn James Anthony is the first person to recognize sensory processing issues as a component of autism.

1700 — 1911 — 1943 — 1944 — 1958

Eugen Bleuler coined the word "autism" to describe children who screened themselves off and were self-absorbed. Autism is derived from the Greek autos (self) and ismos (condition).

Dr. Hans Asperger's described a form of Autism called Asperger's Syndrome. He based his study on a group of 40 children and referred to his patients as "his little professors." He believed that these children exhibited remarkable talents and abilities in specific areas.

There is a controversy over Hans Asperger's cooperation with the Nazi regime. Claims are he may have sent dozens of children to their deaths. Documentation is minimal, with numerous colleagues of Asperger claiming he was a defendant of all children and was investigated twice by the Gestapo for not handing over patients to officials.

Victor Lotter develops a list of behavioral statements for diagnosing autism.

Thousands of teachers are surveyed and Autism is estimated to affect 45 children in 10,000.

In 1980, infantile autism, for the first time, was listed in the DSM-III, separated from childhood schizophrenia. In 1987, infantile Autism in the DSM was replaced by a more expansive definition of Autism that includes diagnostic criteria.

Behavioral Therapy emerges as a Treatment for Autism and is found to be the most successful evidence-based treatment approach for autism spectrum disorder.

The DSM IV is released. It includes subcategories of autism that include:

- Autistic Disorder
- Asperger's Syndrome
- Pervasive Development DIsorder (PDD)

Autism was now coined as a communication disorder.

1965 1977 1980 1981 1994

The Puzzle Piece becomes a symbol for autism because autism is a "puzzling condiction.

Susan Folstein and Sir Michael Rutter published a study on twins in which 21 same-sex twin pairs where at least one of the twins had autism were studied. There was a 36% concordance rate (also known as the heritability statistic) between twins, meaning that if one twin had autism the probability of the identical twin also having autism is 36%.

Lorna Win coined the term "Aspergers Syndrome" after reading an article by Hans Asperger about a milder form of autism. She thought autism should be a broader spectrum of conditions.

What Causes Autism

The cause of Autism is not fully understood, but it is widely believed to be a combination of genetic and environmental factors. Research has identified many genetic variations associated with an increased risk of developing Autism, and some environmental factors, such as infection during pregnancy, have also been linked to the development of Autism.

However, it is essential to note that there is no one cause of Autism and that each individual with Autism may have unique factors that contribute to the development of the condition.

The causes of Autism are incredibly complex and not well understood. Numerous groups have pointed their fingers at different industries, and studies suggest that the combination of genetics, toxins, and pollutants may directly affect the prenatal environment and increase the risk of Autism.

HEREDITARY GENETICS

There is evidence that autism has a genetic component, with many genes associated with an increased risk of developing the condition.

TOXINS AND/OR POLLUTANTS

Environmental factors, such as maternal infection during pregnancy and exposure to certain chemicals, have been linked to an increased risk of autism.

BRAIN DEVELOPMENT

Research suggests that brain development and functioning may be disrupted in individuals with autism, leading to changes in brain structure and function.

INCREASES IN ALLERGIES AND AUTOIMMUNE DISEASES

Studies have indicated an increase in the prevalence of both allergies and Autoimmune diseases over the past few decades, particularly in industrialized nations.

The Blame Game

Blame is a distracting game. I'm not saying we shouldn't try to find the source of autism. Quite the contrary, but often parents are blamed for problematic behaviors, which changes the conversation away from how to address problematic behaviors. We shouldn't try to address the problem because the parents are to blame.

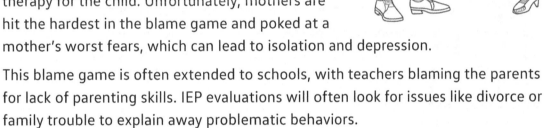

The blame game can also have devastating effects on a marriage. A spouse may blame the other spouse for being the cause of their child's autism and will use that to deflect away from developing an effective

therapy for the child. Unfortunately, mothers are hit the hardest in the blame game and poked at a mother's worst fears, which can lead to isolation and depression.

This blame game is often extended to schools, with teachers blaming the parents for lack of parenting skills. IEP evaluations will often look for issues like divorce or family trouble to explain away problematic behaviors.

THE REFRIGERATOR MOTHER

The refrigerator mother theory is a largely abandoned psychological theory from the the 1950s stated the lack of maternal warmth caused autism. It compares an autistic child to a prisoner in a concentration camp and casts the parents as the guards. Although the theory was widely discredited. Terms like

Parent Induced Autism was still being used in the early 2000s. The "refrigerator mother" theory caused significant harm to families and perpetuated damaging and false beliefs about the cause and treatment of autism.

Historical Treatment of Autism

Attitudes towards autism were very different from what they are today. At that time, autism was not widely understood, and many people believed that it was caused by childhood trauma or emotional problems.

As a result, many children with autism were subjected to various treatments intended to "cure" them of their condition. It is important to note that these practices are no longer considered acceptable and that the scientific community does not support them. Today, children with autism receive a much more supportive and evidence-based approach to treatment, including early intervention, behavioral therapy, and other evidence-based interventions.

INSTITUTIONALIZATION
Many children with autism were placed in institutions where they received little or no educational or therapeutic services. Many of these institutions were overcrowded, understaffed, and poorly equipped to meet the needs of the children.

AVERSIVE THERAPY
Some children with autism were subjected to aversive therapy, which involved the use of physical restraints, shock therapy, punishment, strict diets, and other negative consequences of changing their behavior.

PSYCHOTHERAPY
Some children with autism were subjected to psychotherapy, which was intended to help them understand and overcome the psychological causes of their condition.

DRUG THERAPY
Some children with autism were prescribed drugs to treat their symptoms, but these drugs were often used without clear evidence of their effectiveness, and many had severe side effects.

Lifetime Disability

Autism is considered a lifetime disability. When someone is described as having a lifetime disability, it means that they have a condition or impairment that affects their physical, cognitive, sensory, or emotional abilities. It is expected to persist throughout their entire life.

People with lifetime disabilities may have access to various services and supports to enhance their quality of life and promote their independence. The specific services available can vary depending on their area and individual needs.

MEDICAL AND HEALTHCARE SERVICES

Includes specialized treatments, therapies, medication, and assistive devices.

REHABILITATION SERVICES

Rehabilitation programs aim to enhance abilities through therapies, technologies, and adaptive equipment.

EDUCATION AND VOCATIONAL TRAINING

Specialized education services and vocational training programs

LEGAL AND ADVOCACY SUPPORT

Legal assistance to navigate disability rights and address any discrimination or barriers they may encounter.

SOCIAL AND COMMUNITY SUPPORT

Guidance, advocacy, and assistance in accessing various resources.

HOME AND PERSONAL CARE SERVICES

Assistance with daily living skills such as bathing, dressing, meal preparation, and chores.

TRANSPORTATION SERVICES

Transportation options such as wheelchair-accessible vehicles, handicapped placards, and public transit.

FINANCIAL ASSISTANCE

Government programs, disability benefits, and financial support services can help individuals with lifetime disabilities costs.

Famous People with Autism

Many autistic individuals have excelled in various fields and significantly contributed to society. Some have become successful professionals, entrepreneurs, artists, scientists, advocates, and leaders in their respective fields. Autism can bring unique perspectives, strengths, and talents, such as exceptional attention to detail, intense focus, pattern recognition, creativity, and problem-solving skills. These attributes can be assets in a variety of domains.

It is essential to provide autistic individuals with appropriate support, accommodations, and opportunities for inclusion to enable them to reach their full potential. Recognizing and valuing their strengths, interests, and individuality can help create environments that foster their personal and professional growth. With the right support systems, autistic individuals can overcome challenges and achieve remarkable goals, just like anyone else.

It's also important to remember that autism is a spectrum disorder, and making assumptions about someone's abilities or disabilities based on their public image or personal characteristics can be misleading and harmful.

TEMPLE GRANDIN

Dr. Temple Grandin is a renowned animal behaviorist, autism advocate, and author. She has revolutionized livestock handling and has made significant contributions to the understanding of animal behavior. Temple Grandin has spoken openly about her experiences with autism and has become influential in raising awareness and understanding of the condition.

There are many famous people who are known or suspected to have autism spectrum disorder (ASD). Here are some examples:

NIKOLA TESLA
Inventor

MOZART
Classical Composer

SATOSHI TAJIRI
Creator of Pokémon

EMILY DICKINSON
Poet

ALBERT EINSTEIN
Scientist &
Mathematician

SIR ISAAC NEWTON
Mathematician
and Physicist

THOMAS JEFFERSON
Early American
Politician

BARBARA MCCLINTOCK
Scientist and
Cytogeneticist

TIM BURTON
Movie Director

DAN AYKROYD
Comedic Actor

DARYL HANNAH
Actress & Activist

ANTHONY HOPKINS
Actor

JAMES JOYCE
Author of "Ulysses"

ANDY WARHOL
American Artist

BOBBY FISCHER
Chess Grandmaster

HENRY CAVENDISH
Scientist

THE SECRET AUTISM ROADMAP

Therapies

Parents and therapists, always remember to stay flexible and creative when trying to teach any skill. Dr. Ivar O. Lovaas, says it best:

"If they can't learn the way we teach, we teach the way they learn".

— *Dr. O. Ivar Lovaas, creator of DTT style of ABA*

THE SECRET

The secret is not all early interventions will produce results. Everyone talks about the importance of early interventions, but they don't talk about how some programs are ineffective.

When programs are compared, Intensive at home program ABA programs bring in the best results. Intensive programs that include a mixture of ABA, OT, Speech, and Small Group therapy come in a distant second place. Low-intensity multiple-treatment programs came in the worse, with some skills actually getting worse.

From personal experience, I don't think the second-place option of Intensive programs that included a mixture of ABA, OT, Speech, and Small Group therapy was as effective as the results shown. I felt the main problem was too many people working on issues in different ways, with no one really overseeing the whole program. No one was really involved or invested. Secondly and most importantly, very little to no parent training was involved. Once the therapy ended, nothing was continued in the home. The third issue is that all the therapies were at other people's offices or facilities. Children respond more to people they feel safe with and are more likely to learn in a comfortable environment. The program(s) also needs to be repeatedly reviewed to make sure it is continuing to meet the child's needs.

The second secret is that parent training is just as necessary as the child's therapy. As a parent, you must apply the same techniques the therapist used and start learning how to identify and address new challenges as they occur.

Comparing Therapy Treatment Gains

INTENSIVE ABA ONLY
(30 hours ABA weekly)

INTENSIVE MULTIPLE-TREATMENT
(30 hours weekly, ABA, OT, speech therapy and small group)

LOW INTENSIVE MULTIPLE-TREATMENT
(15 hours weekly combo therapy program, OT, and speech therapy)

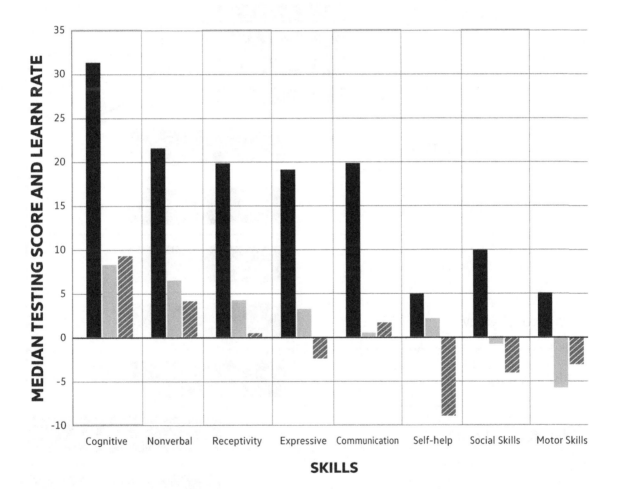

Studies have shown that intensive ABA therapy has great benefits compared to a mixtures of different programs, but it is important to remember not all companies that call themself ABA are true ABA programs. ABA treatment requires high levels of case supervision to ensure effective outcomes.

Eikeseth, S., Smith, T., Jahr, E., & Eldevik, S. (2002). Intensive behavioral treatment at school for 4- to 7-year-old children with autism: A 1-year comparison controlled study. Behavior Modification, 26, 49-68. doi:10.1177/0145445502026001004

Therapies for Every Age

Some therapies are designed for younger children, while others are more effective for issues older children and young adults experience. It's important to note that every child with autism is unique, and what works for one child may not work at that age or work altogether.

	0-2	2-4	5-12	13-21	21+
Child-centric Play Therapy • Early Start Denver Model • RDI • Play Therapy • DIR/Floortime Therapy • Pivotal Response Training	██	██			
Sensory Integration Therapy		██	██		
Speach Therapy		██	██	██	
Occupational Therapy		██	██		
Physical Therapy		██	██		
ABA Therapy		██	██		
Nutritional Therapy			██	██	██
Cognitive Behavior Therapy			██	██	██
Social Skills Training			██	██	██
PEERs				██	

> These programs have many companents that can be quickly and easily be applied in the home.

Who Pays for Therapy

In the United States, early intervention programs for autism are typically funded through a combination of sources. Here are some common funding mechanisms:

INDIVIDUALS WITH DISABILITIES EDUCATION ACT (IDEA)

Part C of the IDEA, known as the Early Intervention Program for Infants and Toddlers with Disabilities provides funding for early intervention services for children from birth to three years old. This federal program ensures that eligible children with developmental delays, including autism, receive appropriate services through Individualized Family Service Plans (IFSPs). Both federal and state governments provide funding.

MEDICAID

Medicaid, a joint federal and state program that provides health coverage for low-income individuals and families, may cover early intervention services for eligible children with autism. Medicaid-funded services can include assessments, therapies, and other interventions. Medicaid eligibility varies by state, and coverage for autism-related services may have specific requirements and limitations.

PRIVATE HEALTH INSURANCE

Many private health insurance plans cover autism-related services, including early intervention programs. The extent and coverage of services vary depending on the insurance plan and state regulations. Coverage may include therapies such as applied behavior analysis (ABA), speech therapy, occupational therapy, and interventions.

OUT-OF-POCKET EXPENSES

Families may choose to pay for early intervention services directly out of pocket. This can involve self-payment for therapy sessions, assessments, and other related services. Sometimes paying for services is done to show they can be effective and then request Health Insurance or School Distircts to pay for them.

SCHOLARSHIPS AND GRANTS

Some families access funding for early intervention programs through scholarships or grants. Eligibility criteria and availability vary depending on the organization providing the funding.

What are the Goals of Early Intervention?

Every child is different, but this is a starting point on what areas of need are commonly addressed in early intervention.

SOCIAL LANGUAGE
- Receptive
- Expressives
- Echoics

PLAY SKILLS
- Pretend
- Interactive
- Cause & Effect
- Parallel Play

SOCIAL SKILLS
- Self Esteem
- Social Interaction
- Social Language
- Conflict Resolution
- Social Rules

DAILY LIVING SKILLS
- Safety
- Home Skills
- Community
- Personal

GOALS
- Teach new and meaningful skills
- Maximize independent living
- Reduce challenging behaviors
- Train parents to be their kid's best teacher

COGNITION
- Emotions · Sarcasm
- Thinking · Desires
- Perspective Taking
- Preferencess

MOTOR SKILLS
- Visual
- Fine
- Gross
- Oral

ACADEMIC SKILLS
- Literacy
- Mathematics
- Organizing
- Planning

EXECUTIVE FUNCTIONING
- Attention & Focus
- Memory · Flexibility
- Problem Solving
- Planning

What Skills Do Each Therapy Address

Every individual is unique, and the best approach to supporting them will depend on their specific strengths, challenges, and goals of that person. Different therapies have different approaches, and different terminologies. Developing the best therapy program requires ongoing work. Still, studies have shown that one of the worst things that can happen is having multiple programs trying to achieve similar goals in different ways. This can cause the child to feel resentment and frustration toward therapy.

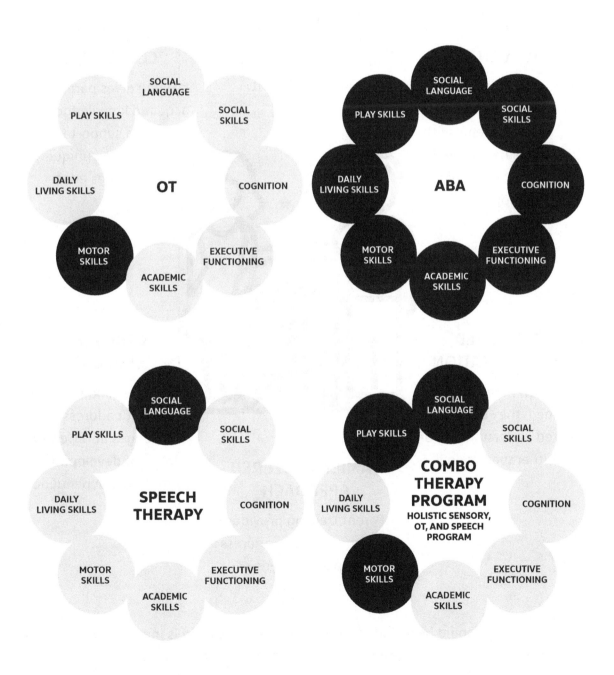

Parent Training

Parent training is one of the most critical aspects of addressing autism. It gives parents the ability to acquire the necessary skills and strategies to support their child's development and manage challenging behaviors at home and in the environment in which they live.

CONSISTENCY AND GENERALIZATION

Parent training helps ensure consistency in implementing strategies across different settings.

EARLY INTERVENTION

Parent training enables early intervention by equipping parents with the necessary knowledge to support their child's development.

INCREASED CONFIDENCE

Training gives parents the acquired knowledge and skills to support their child when unique challenges arise.

INCREASED COLLABORATION

When parents are trained, they develop a shared understanding of the therapeutic goal.

LONG-TERM SUPPORT

Parent training provides tools for addressing challenges at different stages of development, promoting independence.

FAMILY-CENTERED APPROACH

Parent training provides an opportunity to address the specific needs of the family.

Parent training should be included with any therapy the child is involved with. This ensures the strategies and supports provided in therapy are continued.

Parental training is essential to making any program more successful. There are numerous ways to receive parental training:

WORKSHOPS AND CONFERENCES

These events often feature expert speakers, panel discussions, and interactive sessions.

SUPPORT GROUPS AND ORGANIZATIONS

These groups provide opportunities to connect with other parents, share experiences, and learn from one another.

ONLINE RESOURCES, VIDEOS & WEBINARS

There is a wealth of information, articles, and videos online.

ONLINE FORUMS AND SOCIAL MEDIA

These platforms allow parents to connect with other families, ask questions and share experiences.

PARENT TRAINING PROGRAMS

Workshops, courses, and one-on-one consultations to equip parents with knowledge on autism subjects.

BOOKS AND LITERATURE

Numerous books offer valuable insights into autism and practical guidance for parents.

Early Intervention Using Child-Centric Play-based Therapy

GREAT FOR VERY EARLY INTERVENTION

Parents or caregivers often might suspect a child has Autism, but they are too young to get an official diagnosis or have a diagnosis. Still, they are waiting to start a therapy program. Child Centric Play-based therapy is a great way to turn every interaction with the child into an enjoyable therapy session at home.

A few early intervention therapy sessions take place on the child's level, literally and metaphorically. The therapist or parents meets the young child at their level, physically by sitting on the floor, and emotionally and by developing meaningful interactions by following their lead in play-based interactions.

The best know of these therapies are:
- **DIR/FLOORTIME THERAPY**
- **EARLY START DENVER MODEL (ESDM)**
- **PIVOTAL RESPONSE TRAINING (PRT)**
- **RELATIONSHIP DEVELOPMENT INTERVENTION**

These therapies focus on:

- **NATURALISTIC TEACHING:** This uses play-based activities to teach the child new skills in a natural, non-threatening environment.

- **JOINT ATTENTION:** Joint attention refers to the ability to share awareness with others and is a critical skill for social communication.

- **UNDERSTANDING EMOTIONS:** Emotional sharing is the ability to express and understand emotions in oneself and others.

- **VISUAL SUPPORTS:** Visual supports, such as picture schedules or visual cues, can help the child understand and follow routines and instructions. Also, give your child choices to help them feel empowered and motivated.

- **POSITIVE REINFORCEMENT:** Positive reinforcement encourages the child to engage in desired behaviors. This might involve providing praise or a small rewards, such as a sticker or a favorite toy, when the child completes a task or activity.

TIPS

Early Intervention Using Child Centric Play-based Therapy

There are several techniques that parents can use to implement Child Centric Play-based Therapy at home. Here are some suggestions:

ENCOURAGE COMMUNICATION
Use simple language, gestures, and visual cues to help your child understand and express their thoughts, feelings, and needs.

JOIN IN THEIR WORLD
Engage in activities that your child enjoys and finds meaningful.

FOLLOW YOUR CHILD'S LEAD

EXPAND AND EXTEND PLAY
Once your child is engaged in a particular activity, gradually introduce new elements or ideas to expand their play.

FOSTER EMOTIONAL CONNECTIONS
Use facial expressions, body language, and tone of voice to convey empathy, understanding, and support.

PRACTICE TURN-TAKING AND SOCIAL SKILLS

BE FLEXIBLE AND PATIENT

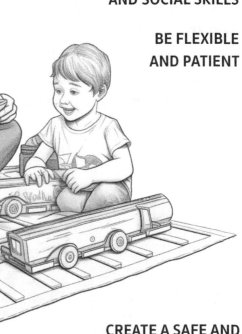

USE SENSORY ACTIVITIES
Provide opportunities for your child to explore different textures, sounds, smells, tastes, and movements through sensory play.

CREATE A SAFE AND ENGAGING ENVIRONMENT
Set up a dedicated play area in you are free from distractions and provides a variety of toys and materials that capture your child's interest.

Play Therapy as the Child Grows

Play therapy can also be used as the child grows older. Play therapy aims to create a safe and supportive environment for the individual to learn, explore, and practice social skills and emotional regulation engagingly and enjoyably. Play-based activities are tailored to the individual's interests and strengths to build connections with them and facilitate learning.

Play therapy can benefit all ages by providing a safe and supportive environment for developing vital social, communication, and emotional skills.

FOR YOUNG CHILDREN

Play-based activities can be particularly effective in developing communication, social, and emotional skills. Play therapy can help children learn to express themselves, regulate their emotions, and interact with others in a fun and engaging way.

FOR OLDER CHILDREN

Play therapy can still be effective, but the therapist may incorporate more structured activities and exercises to target specific social skills, problem areas, and communication skills.

FOR ADULTS

Play therapy can be adapted to focus on developing vocational and life skills, such as interview skills, job training, problem-solving, and stress management.

TIPS Play Therapy as the Child Grows

Play therapy is a therapeutic approach that utilizes play as a means of communication and self-expression for children with autism. There are several techniques that parents can use to implement Play Therapy at home. Here are some suggestions:

CREATE A SAFE AND SUPPORTIVE PLAY ENVIRONMENT
Set up a designated play area in your home. Ensure that the space is free from distractions and provides toys and materials that stimulate your child's interests.

FOLLOW YOUR CHILD'S LEAD

ENCOURAGE SYMBOLIC PLAY

INCORPORATE SENSORY EXPERIENCES

USE VISUAL SUPPORTS

BE FLEXIBLE AND PATIENT

ENCOURAGE SYMBOLIC ROLE PLAY
Symbolic play involves using objects or actions to represent something else.

FOSTER SOCIAL INTERACTION:
Provide opportunities for your child to engage in social play experiences with siblings, peers, or family members.

SPECIFIC GOALS
Identify specific goals, such as fine motor skills, turn-taking skills, improving communication, following multistep instructions, and emotional regulation.

Sensory Integration Therapy

Sensory Integration Therapy is an approach to help sensory processing difficulties effectively process and respond to sensory information from their environment. The therapy seeks to improve sensory integration, enhance sensory processing skills, and support self-regulation through various activities and exercises, such as swinging, brushing, and tactile play. By addressing difficulties related to sensory processing, this therapy aims to improve an individual's ability to engage, interact, and participate in daily activities, ultimately enhancing their overall functioning and quality of life.

Addressing sensory integration issues in children can have several significant benefits. Here are a few:

ENHANCING DAILY FUNCTIONING
Sensory integration difficulties can significantly impact a person's ability to engage in everyday activities. By addressing these issues, individuals can improve their ability to participate in self-care tasks, school-related activities, and leisure activities.

PROMOTING ATTENTION AND FOCUS
Addressing sensory integration issues can help improve attention and reduce distractibility.

SUPPORTING SOCIAL INTERACTION
Sensory difficulties can affect a person's ability to engage in social interactions and form meaningful relationships.

IMPROVING EMOTIONAL REGULATION
Sensory integration difficulties can contribute to emotional dysregulation, leading to heightened anxiety, irritability, or meltdowns.

ENHANCING MOTOR SKILLS AND COORDINATION
Sensory integration is closely linked to motor development and coordination. Difficulties in processing sensory input can affect a person's ability to coordinate movements, maintain balance, or develop fine motor skills.

INCREASING OVERALL WELL-BEING
When sensory integration challenges are addressed, individuals may experience reduced sensory-related discomfort, anxiety, and frustration.

TIPS Improving Sensory Integration

It is important to create a sensory lifestyle or activity plan. Improving sensory integration at home can help reduce anxiety and relax your child. Here are some exercises and activities parents can do at home to promote sensory integration:

SWINGING OR SPINNING

Swinging or spinning can have a calming effect and improve balance and coordination.

MUSIC THERAPY

Encourage your child to engage in activities like dancing, clapping, or playing instruments.

SENSORY WALKS

Take your child for sensory walks. Encourage them to touch different textures, listen, and look around.

DEEP PRESSURE

Deep pressure can help promote a sense of calm and improve body awareness.

SENSORY BINS

Create sensory bins filled with materials like rice, beans, or sand.

YOGA OR STRETCHING

Practice gentle yoga poses or stretching exercises with your child.

GROSS MOTOR

Encourage jumping on a trampoline, playing catch, or doing animal walks.

SCENTED ACTIVITIES

Introduce scented markers, scented playdough or fragrant bubbles.

WATER PLAY

Go swimming or set up water play activities using a small pool.

Sensory Issues

Sensory issues are common in people with autism and can significantly impact their daily lives. These sensory issues arise from differences in how the brain processes and responds to sensory information. Understanding and addressing sensory issues are crucial in supporting the child's overall development and well-being. Occupational therapists and other professionals trained in sensory integration techniques can work to identify their specific sensory challenges and develop personalized strategies to help them better process and respond to sensory stimuli.

Auditory Sensitivity

AUDITORY HYPERSENSITIVITY: Startled by loud noises cover their ears in response to certain sounds, or find background noises overwhelming.

AUDITORY HYPOSENSITIVITY: May not respond to their name being called, seem unresponsive to specific sounds or even seek out loud noises.

Visual Sensitivity

VISUAL HYPERSENSITIVITY: Bright lights or busy visual environments may cause discomfort or distress.

VISUAL HYPOSENSITIVITY: May engage in repetitive behaviors such as watching moving objects or flicking their fingers in front of their eyes.

Taste and Smell Sensitivity

They may be extremely sensitive to tastes, flavors, or smelsl and could have react strongly to certain foods they eat.

Vestibular Hyposensitivity

Seeks out intense movement experiences, such as spinning or jumping.

Crowds and Social Interaction

Social situations can be overwhelming for individuals with autism due to the complexity of sensory input, social cues, and expectations.

Tactile Hyposensitivity

They might seek deep pressure or engage in self-stimulatory behaviors like hand-flapping or spinning. Clothing sensitivity can also occur with certain fabrics, seams, tags, or clothing materials that may feel uncomfortable.

Self-Injurious Behavior

May engage in self-injurious behaviors, such as head-banging, hand-biting, or hitting themselves. These behaviors can response to sensory overload, frustration, anxiety, or difficulty in expressing emotions.

Repetitive Behaviors

Often referred to as "stimming," it involves repetitive movements or actions, such as hand-flapping, rocking, spinning, or lining up objects.

Sensory Avoidance

May actively avoid specific ssensory experiences or environments. For example, they might avoid crowded places, loud events, or overwhelming environments.

Sensory Seeking

May actively seek out intense sensory experiences such as body pressure, spinning, or swinging. They can also seek out other sensory needs that should be addressed quickly before they become dangerous or self-injurious.

PICA: Pica is a behavior where individuals have a strong desire to eat non-food items. This can include dirt, paper, rocks, hair, or even inedible objects. Pica can be dangerous, as ingesting non-food items can lead to gastrointestinal problems, choking hazards, and other health issues.

SMEARING: Smearing refers to the spreading or smearing feces. This behavior can be distressing for caregivers and is often related to sensory issues.

ELOPEMENT: Elopement, also known as wandering, is when a child wanders or runs off. This behavior can be dangerous and puts the individual at risk of getting lost, injured, or encountering hazardous situations.

Speech Therapy

Speech therapy can be benefit individuals with Autism Spectrum Disorder (ASD) of all ages, from toddlers to adults. The specific techniques and activities used in therapy sessions will vary depending on the age and developmental level of the individual.

FOR YOUNG CHILDREN with ASD, speech therapy can be particularly effective in developing communication skills, including spoken language, gestures, and social communication. Play-based activities, visual aids, and social stories help the child learn new vocabulary, sentence structure, and social communication skills.

FOR OLDER CHILDREN and adolescents with ASD, speech therapy can focus on more advanced communication skills, such as conversation skills, pragmatic language, and perspective-taking. Role-playing and video modeling help the child practice these skills in a structured and supportive environment.

FOR ADULTs with ASD, speech therapy can be adapted to focus on de eloping communication skills for work and social situations. The therapist may use conversation analysis, video feedback, and social coaching to help the individual develop practical communication skills and navigate social interactions.

Exercises and Activities

ARTICULATING ACTIVITIES: These activities will help the child slowly pronounce each word by demonstrating and making specific sounds during playtime or fun activities.

LANGUAGE ACTIVITIES: These activities will get the child involved in talking by using visual methods like pictures, books, and objects that can help stimulate the development of the language.

FACIAL EXERCISES: Facial exercises may help strengthen the muscles around the mouth. In addition, the Speech Therapist may employ a variety of tongue, jaw, and lip movement exercises.

TIPS Encouraging Speech

Several activities can help promote speech Here are some ideas:

CREATE A DISTRACTION-FREE AREA

Set up a designated play area in your home. Ensure it is free from distraction.

SOCIAL STORIES

Social stories help explain social situations, and explain how to deal with them while improving the language.

ROLE-PLAYING

Role-playing can be a fun way identify social cues and improve communication skills.

GAMES

Games like "20 Questions" can be a fun and engaging way to practice and engage in communication.

SINGING AND MUSIC

Singing and music can be a great way to encourage speech and language. While helping with rhythm, intonation, and pronunciation.

STORYTELLING

Storytelling can help develop language skills and creativity. A child can create their own stories or explain what is or will happen in a picture.

ARTICULATION EXERCISES

Articulation exercises can help develop speech sounds and pronunciation. This can include repeating sounds and practicing tongue twisters.

Breaking Down Conversations Skills

Conversation skills are complicated, but if you break conversations down, you can start by focusing on greetings and salutations and then asking questions. Here are some tips and techniques that can be helpful:

- **VISUAL SUPPORTS:** Create visual cards or pictures depicting greetings or salutations.

- **SOCIAL STORIES:** Create a social story focused on greetings and salutations, highlighting the steps involved and expected responses.

- **MODEL THE BEHAVIOR:** Model greetings in various situations and with different people to help them understand when and where to use them.

- **REINFORCEMENT:** When the individual initiates or responds to a greeting appropriately, provide praise, a smile, or a small reward as positive reinforcement.

- **PRACTICE IN SAFE ENVIRONMENT:** Begin teaching greetings in a controlled and familiar environment where the individual feels comfortable and relaxed.

- **ROLE-PLAYING:** Engage in role-playing scenarios where you and the individual take turns practicing greetings with each other or with other familiar people.

- **PEER MODELING:** Involve neurotypical peers, in person or in videos, to model appropriate greetings.

- **BE PATIENT AND UNDERSTANDING:** Be patient, celebrate small successes, and don't get discouraged if progress seems slow.

- **USE SOCIAL GAMES:** Incorporate games and activities that involve greetings, such as "Simon Says" or role-playing games with dolls or action figures.

Staying on Track

Keeping a conversation on track can be challenging due to difficulties in social communication and understanding nonverbal cues.

- **USE VISUAL SUPPORTS:** Visual supports like conversation cue cards or flowcharts can be helpful. These tools can outline the steps of a conversation and provide cues for turn-taking, active listening, and topic maintenance.

- **TEACH TURN-TAKING:** Explicitly teach the concept of turn-taking or asking questions during conversations.

- **INCORPORATE INTERESTS:** Use the child's special interests in the conversation topics. Talking about subjects they are passionate about can increase their engagement and focus.

- **USE VISUAL TIMERS:** If the conversation is time-limited, use a visual timer to indicate the duration of the conversation. This can help the individual understand when the exchange will end.

- **PRACTICE CONVERSATIONS:** Engage in role-playing or social skills training sessions to practice conversations in a safe and supportive environment.

TIPS Improving Fine Motor Skills (OT)

Occupational therapists work to develop the fine motor skills needed to be functional in a school and home setting. From grasping a pencil to putting together Legos, fine motor skills are the coordination of small muscles in movement with the eyes, hands, and fingers

Here are some exercises children can do at home to improve fine motor skills:

PLAYDOUGH ACTIVITIES
Encourage your child to roll, pinch, and shape the dough.

PUZZLES AND BUILDING BLOCKS
These promote hand-eye coordination, finger control, and spatial awareness.

THREADING AND LACING
Threading or lacing items improves hand-eye coordination.

CUTTING AND TEARING
Provide old magazines or newspapers for them to cut or tear.

SORTING AND STACKING
Stack small objects like buttons, coins, or beads, and ask them to sort and stack them based on different attributes such as color, shape, or size.

COLORING AND DRAWING
These activities promote hand control, precision, and creativity.

TWEEZERS OR TONGS ACTIVITIES
Pick up the objects using the tweezers or tongs.

TRACING AND WRITING
Help your child practice tracing shapes or letters. Gradually progress to writing activities, allowing them to practice forming letters or words.

POURING AND SCOOPING
Practice pouring or scooping, which helps improve hand-eye coordination and fine motor control.

TIPS Improving Gross Motor Skills (OT)

Gross motor skills involve movements of the large muscles of the arms, legs, and body. They include body awareness, physical strength, and reaction time. An essential part of OT is creating a sensory lifestyle or activity plan. It aims to incorporate sensory activities throughout the child's day to improve focus and attention and ensure the child feels "just right" (regulated) throughout the day.

Parents can set up a safe area and home and do many exercises that can help to improve gross motor skills.

OBSTACLE COURSE
Create a mini obstacle course in your home using pillows, cushions, and other safe objects.

ANIMAL WALKS
Encourage your child to imitate animal movements such as crab walks, frog jumps, or bunny hops.

SIMON SAYS
Play the classic game of Simon Says with gross motor movements.

DANCE PARTY
Put on some energetic music and have a dance party with your child.

BALLOON VOLLEYBALL
Inflate a balloon and play volleyball with your child.

JUMPING JACKS
Start with more straightforward modifications like clapping hands above the head.

HULA HOOPING
Give your child a hula hoop and encourage them to twirl it around their waist or arms.

SCAVENGER HUNTS
Create a scavenger hunt round the house and collect specific items.

YOGA
Practice simple yoga poses together with your child.

ABA

Applied Behavior Analysis

ABA is widely considered to be the gold standard for autism treatment. You can do an internet search for "ABA" and "gold standard" and get hundreds of results. That's because ABA therapy for autism has been studied for decades and possesses the largest body of research supporting it.

The benefits of ABA therapy are substantial and backed up by many long-term studies. Most experts consider it the gold-standard treatment for children with autism spectrum disorder (ASD) that can drastically improve social, communication, and learning skills.

ABA doesn't do it alone. Parents must become fluent enough in the basics of behavioral intervention to apply the principles and techniques at home. A behavioral therapist might work 10-20 hours a week with your child, but that is a small amount of time that you will be interacting with your child.

ABA is most effective when done regularly in the home. Children often learn quickest where they are comfortable. Therapy at home also allows parents to observe and participate. Skills are also generalized quicker.

Addressing Areas of Need

When done right, ABA can address numerous categories. It is important to note that the central premise of an ABA program is teaching a child "how to learn" so that they will no longer need such structured and specialized services.

ABA therapy emphasizes the modification of behaviors by utilizing strategies such as prompting, shaping, reinforcement, and fading to encourage desired behaviors.

It is based on data collection and analysis to guide treatment decisions by tracking the effectiveness of interventions and making informed adjustments as needed.

To ensure behaviors stick, ABA aims to promote generalizing newly learned skills across different settings. It also focuses on maintenance, ensuring that acquired skills are retained over time.

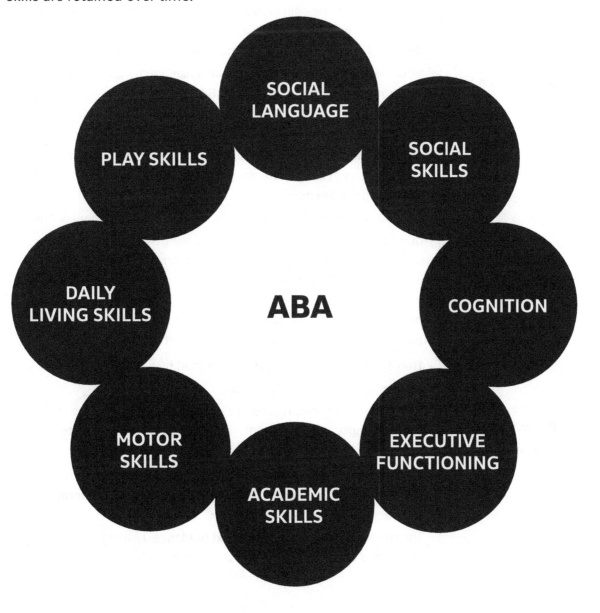

Not all ABA Programs are the Same.

Unfortunately, the name ABA is often used by therapy programs that utilize some of the elements of ABA. Still, it realistically wouldn't be considered an ABA program or at least a good program.

Program Supervision	An ABA BCBA (Applied Behavior Analysis Board Certified Behavior Analyst) is a professional who has completed training and received a BCBA, which certifies they are specialized in applied behavior analysis (ABA) therapy and interventions. · Will conduct assessments to understand the behavior. · Based on the assessments, BCBA's develop individualized Behavior Intervention Plans. · BCBAs analyze the collected data on behaviors and interventions to measure progress. They use this data to make informed decisions and modify the treatment plan. · BCBAs often provide training and supervision to behavior technicians or paraprofessionals. They teach ABA techniques and ensure that interventions are implemented correctly and consistently. · BCBAs collaborate with parents, caregivers, teachers, and other professionals. They provide guidance, support, and training to help implement ABA strategies across different settings, such as home, school, or community. · BCBAs may be involved in behavior support and crisis management. · BCBAs adhere to a code of ethics that maintains standards that ensure their practice is evidence-based, prioritize the clients' well-being, and maintain confidentiality.
Behavioral Therapist	A behavioral therapist is crucial in implementing the therapy program interventions and working directly with the child. · They follow the treatment plan designed by a BCBA. · Applies specific ABA techniques. · The behavioral therapist engage in 1on1 sessions with the child, using prompts, reinforcement, and shaping techniques to teach new skills. · Collects data on the treatment plan. · Collaborates with parents to ensure consistency and generalize skills across different settings. · The therapist provides support and guidance, helping navigate challenges and promote progress in areas of development.

ABA Home-Based Programs	ABA program is provided in the home where the child feels the most comfortable. • Parents can observe, learn and participate in the therapy. • Skills can be generalized the environment.
ABA Center-Based Programs	ABA program is provided in a facility (center-based) that conducts a series of planned socialization or activities. • Programs aren't usually individualized to the child's needs. • Goals aren't usually generalized to the child's actual environment. • Programs don't usually have parent training or communication.
ABA School-Based Programs	ABA program is provided in the school setting. • Therapists are often poorly trained and don't follow ABA protocols. • Programs usually lack parental training and communication. • Programs are extremely slow to adapt or change as needed or respond to a crisis. • Programs don't generalize skills to the home or community.
Parent Training	Parent training is essential in an ABA program as it promotes consistency, generalization of skills, and continuity of care. • Consistency in implementing interventions enhances learning opportunities and promotes generalization of skills. • Parents' continuity of care can lead to lasting progress. • Training empowers parents to actively modify strategies. • Ensures Long-Term Sustainability
Positive Reinforcements	ABA should be a positive experience. A common autism trait is a strong interest in subjects. Those interests can be a great motivator by providing rewards that are of interest. That doesn't mean taking away a toy until a child learns a behavior but instead earning a new toy.
Poorly Trained Therapist	Poorly trained or just bad therapists can be emotionally or physically abusive. Their technique will go outside of ABA guidelines, and they will often try to pursue punishment as their methods fail.
Easily Adaptable	Every individual is unique, with different strengths, challenges, and learning styles. ABA programs should be tailored to the specific needs of each individual to maximize their progress. Programs require flexibility and must be adapted and modified to address different skills, environments, or challenges.

How Does ABA Work?

ABA therapy utilizes scientifically proven techniques to address problematic behaviors and teach new behaviors to empower individuals to reach their fullest potential in various aspects of life.

A <u>BEHAVIORAL INTERVENTION</u> PLAN IS FORMATED.

The program manager will have a BCBA certification. They will do a Functional Behavioral Analysis to find the Why, Where, and When of a behavior They will then utilize Evidence Based principals to develop a Behavioral Intervention Plan to address the behavior.

DATA IS COLLECTED ON THE BEHAVIOR.

Data collection types are:

Frequency: How often it happens
Rate: How often it occurs in an hour.
Duration: How long a behavior happened.
Latency: How long it took the child to do the right behavior.

THE <u>ABCS OF THE BEHAVIOR</u>

Behaviors are analyzed.

A = ANTICIDENTS
What happens before the behavior?

B = BEHAVIORAL
The behavior is a result of the antecedent.

C = CONSEQUENCE
What happens after the behavior?

<u>TEACHING STRATEGIES</u> ARE APPLIED.

Discrete Trial: The student is given instructions and is rewarded for doing that behavior. The reward is individualized per student.

Naturalistic Teaching: Uses guidance for social skills.

Token Economy: Uses tokens that can be collected for a reward.

Contingent Observation: If a child is disruptive, they can be removed from the environment.

A <u>TASK ANALYSIS</u> BREAKS DOWN A SKILLS INTO MANAGEABLE TASKS.

1: Identify Skill
2: Determine the Skills Needed
3: Break down skills
4: Test the breakdown.
5: Teach the skill through videos, pictures, or real life.
6: Assess the skill.

THERAPIES WILL IMPLEMENT VARIOUS <u>ABA COMPONENTS</u> TO ADDRESS BEHAVIORS.

SHAPPING
Gradually modify an existing behavior to a new desired behavior.

FADING
Prompts are reduced until they are no longer used.

EFFECTIVE
Can see results.

PROMPTING
• Gestural Prompts
• Verbal Prompts
• Positional Prompts
• Visual Prompts
• Physical prompts

GENERALIZATION
Generalize skills into different environments with different people.

EXTINCTION
Reinforcements for problematic behaviors are removed.

REWARDS
Rewarding positive behavior works.

HOME-BASED
Child is more comfortable learning at home.

ADAPTIVE
Programs adjust quickly to concerns or lack of progress.

PROGRAMS WILL BE CONSTANTLY MONITORED WITH DATA COLLECTION AND REVIEWS.

• ABA therapists collect data to track progress, evaluate treatment effectiveness, and data inform decision-making to develop and improve the program.
• Behaviors are also monitored for Environmental Stimulas and Reinforcementas.

Breaking Down Complex Tasks

Breaking down complex tasks is a critical strategy used to facilitate learning and skill development. Breaking down a task into smaller steps makes it easier to process, organize and perform the task. This reduces overwhelming a person and enhances learning by targeting specific skills one at a time.

Task: Brushing Teeth

STEPS:

- **A** Pick up the toothbrush.
- **B** Squeeze toothpaste onto the toothbrush.
- **C** Put the toothpaste back in its place.
- **D** Bring the toothbrush to the mouth and start brushing the teeth in a circular motion.
- **E** Spit out the toothpaste into the sink.
- **F** Rinse the mouth with water and spit it out.

Task: Getting Dressed

STEPS:

- **A** Pick out clean clothes to wear.
- **B** Take off pajamas or current clothes.
- **C** Put on underwear and socks.
- **D** Put on pants or a skirt.
- **E** Put on a shirt or blouse.
- **F** If applicable, put on a sweater or jacket.
- **G** Put on shoes and tie shoelaces.

Task: Completing a Worksheet

STEPS:

- **A** Read the instructions.
- **B** Look at the first problem and read it carefully.
- **C** Use a pencil to solve the problem step by step.
- **D** Check the answer and make corrections.
- **E** Move on to the next problem and repeat the steps.

Extinction Isn't Just For Diansaurs

In ABA, extinction is a behavioral procedure to reduce or eliminate undesirable behaviors. It involves withholding reinforcement to decrease the occurrence of that behavior over time. Positive reinforcements can be used when the new appropriate behavior is achieved.

Mouthing Objects (Pica)

BEHAVIOR: A child frequently puts non-food objects in their mouth as a sensory-seeking behavior.

EXTINCTION: Systematically reduce access to objects the child tends to mouth and redirect them to more appropriate sensory activities.

Repetitive Questioning

BEHAVIOR: A teenager repeatedly asks the same question even after receiving an answer.

EXTINCTION: Use a planned ignoring approach, meaning they stop responding to the repetitive questions while reinforcing appropriate communication skills and seeking alternative ways to express their needs or interests.

Picky Eating

BEHAVIOR: A child engages in selective eating, refusing to eat certain foods.

EXTINCTION: Stop giving attention or offering preferred foods when the child refuses to eat particular foods. Encourage and reinforce trying new foods while ensuring a balanced and appropriate diet.

Prompting

Prompting assists individuals in successfully completing tasks or acquiring new skills. It involves providing cues or hints to guide the individual's behavior toward the desired response or correct action. The goal of prompting is to facilitate learning and increase the chances of a correct response until the individual can perform the skill independently.

Prompting strategies are often implemented gradually, starting with more intrusive prompts and fading them over time so the person becomes more independent and proficient in the task. The ultimate goal of prompting is enabling the individual to perform the behavior or task without assistance, promoting independence and functional skills.

PHYSICAL PROMPTS

These are the most intrusive prompts and involve physically guiding the child through the correct sequence of actions.

GESTURAL PROMPTS

Gestural prompts involve hand gestures or non-verbal cues to direct the individual's attention to the relevant stimuli or action.

VERBAL PROMPTS

Verbal prompts include giving verbal instructions or cues to guide the child's behavior.

VISUAL PROMPTS

Visual prompts use visual aids or cues to support learning and prompt the desired behavior. This can include showing pictures, using written instructions, or displaying step-by-step visual guides.

MODELING PROMPTS

Modeling prompts involve demonstrating the desired behavior or skill for the individual to imitate.

Is it a Reward, or is it Bribery?

When using rewards or incentives, it is essential to use them in a structured way that supports a designed campaign to learn a new behavior or extinguish a problematic behavior.

REWARD

HAS LONG-TERM POSITIVE CHANGES

A reword is used as a reinforcement. It is part of a structured adult-led plan. It follows good behavior and is delivered with praise and encouragement.

BRIBERY

ENCOURAGES NEGATIVE BEHAVIORS

Bribery is not used as a reinforcement. It is not planned out. It is a reactive response that encourages negative behaviors. It doesn't follow a consistent pattern and is given under duress to stop a behavior immediately.

Toilet Training 6-Step Plan

Toilet training a child with autism can be a bit more challenging, but it is definitely possible with patience, consistency, and understanding. Every child is unique so the approach may vary depending on the individual needs and sensitivities of the child.

1 Introduction

Assess if your child is physically and emotionally ready for toilet training.

2 Demonstrate with a Toy or Stuffed Animal

Children learn better by watching others. Demonstrate with a toy or stuffed animal and have them walk through the toileting process.

3 Use Visual Guide

Create a visual schedule or a picture-based step-by-step guide to help them understand the process.

4 Sit on Potty

Establish a consistent schedule for toilet breaks. Take your child to the bathroom regularly, even if they may not indicate the need to go.

5 Encourage and Reward

Praise and reward your child when they use the toilet successfully. Positive reinforcement can motivate them to repeat the behavior.

Incorporate your child's special interests into the toilet training process. For example, consider using themed underwear or potty training materials if they love a cartoon character.

6 Keep on a Schedule

Establish a consistent schedule for toilet breaks. Take your child to the bathroom regularly, even if they may not indicate the need to go.

Celebrate each milestone and continue to work patiently with your child. With consistent effort and understanding, toilet training can become a successful and positive experience for both of you. Remember, accidents are a part of the learning process. Avoid punishment or scolding for accidents, as it may create anxiety and hinder progress. Stay patient, calm, and supportive throughout the process.

Frustration and Anger Management

Frustration and anger management requires a comprehensive and individualized approach considering the child's unique needs and sensitivity.

Monitor and Reduce Triggers

Identify triggers that lead to frustration and try to minimize their impact. If certain situations consistently lead to anger, finding ways to avoid or modify those situations can be helpful.

Teach Emotional Awareness

Help the child recognize and identify their emotions. Use visual aids or emotion cards to help them understand and express their feelings.

Implement Calm-Down Techniques

Teach the child calming strategies, such as deep breathing exercises, counting to ten, or using a quiet space where they can go to relax when overwhelmed.

Social Stories

Use social stories or narratives to explain everyday frustrating situations and appropriate ways to react. Social stories can help explain how to handle situations.

Offer Choices and Control

Provide the child with choices and opportunities for control when appropriate. This can empower them and reduce frustration when they may feel powerless.

Use Visual Supports

Visual schedules, timers, or checklists can help the child understand the sequence of activities and manage their time, reducing frustration.

Model and Practice Problem-Solving

Demonstrate problem-solving techniques and encourage the child to practice them. This can help them find constructive ways to address their frustrations.

Positive Reinforcement

Praise and reward the child when they handle frustrating situations well. Positive reinforcement can motivate them to continue using appropriate coping strategies.

Questions to Ask to Find a Good ABA Program

Many agencies are saying they have an ABA program, but only a few agencies offer true ABA programs that are effective. True ABA programs have program managers and BCBAs that develop a program based on the child's needs. The parents and caregiver work with the program manager and therapist on the program in different environments (home, school, and community). Most importantly, only positive reinforcements are used.

ABA programs are designed to be very flexible, with constant data tracking, planning, and ongoing assessments. The parents and caregiver are trained in the methodology, and the therapists receive extensive training before and ongoing. Team meetings happen regularly, including all therapists, parents, and caregivers. Sometimes, you will have a therapist who isn't suitable for the program, and they will need to switch them out quickly.

Before you start an ABA program, these questions should be asked:

- How many BCBAs do you have on staff?
- Who will be determining the goals and program for my child? Do you consider input from parents?
- How many behavioral therapists do you have?
- How many therapists will be working with my child?
- What sort of training do your therapists receive? How often?
- How much direct supervision do therapists receive from the BCBAs weekly?
- What does a typical ABA session look like?
- Do you offer home-based or clinic-based therapy?
- How is progress evaluated?
- How often do you re-evaluate goals?
- How is parent/caretaker training conducted?
- How many hours per week can you provide?

Is ABA Therapy Harmful?

Lately, there have been some complaints that ABA can cause trauma. ABA's goal is to guide a person to use appropriate behaviors so they can have the best chance at making their way through life. Parents, BCBAs, and therapists, most likely, had the child's best interest at heart. It is extremely tough to have a child get lost in themself. Bite themself or bang their head against a wall when they get frustrated, have Uncontrolled fits if their shirt is uncomfortable, or they run out into a street full of traffic because they want to escape a situation, or they aren't paying attention.

Most of the complaints about ABA appear when an agency or school provides some sort of therapy or service and calls it ABA. Still, when the program is evaluated, it doesn't follow the ABA model.

OVEREMPHASIS ON COMPLIANCE: Critics argue that ABA therapy can place excessive emphasis on compliance and obedience, focusing on behaviors that are considered socially acceptable. They contend that this approach may negatively impact an individual's self-esteem and mental well-being.

LACK OF GENERALIZATION: Some argue that ABA therapy can be overly focused on discrete skills and behaviors, leading to challenges in generalizing these skills to different settings, contexts, and individuals.

ETHICAL CONCERNS: Critics raise ethical considerations for ABA therapy, particularly regarding punishment and aversive techniques. While modern ABA approaches prioritize positive reinforcement, some individuals express concerns about physical prompts or withholding reinforcement.

LACK OF INDIVIDUALIZATION: Critics argue that ABA therapy can sometimes ignore a person's personality. They contend that a more personality-centered approach may be better suited to their unique strengths.

All of these complaints are not an issue in good ABA programs. It is important to remember many programs use the term ABA, but in reality, they don't follow the best practices of ABA, so it is imperative to be involved with any program your child is a part of.

 WARNING: It is extremely important to pay close attention to a therapist or anyone working closely with your child in a one-on-one setting. That includes therapists, instructors, aides, or teachers.

Social Skills Training

Autism, social skills training, refers to a type of intervention that focuses on developing and improving the social skills of individuals on the autism spectrum. It is designed to help individuals with autism better navigate social interactions, understand social cues, and establish meaningful relationships with others.

The specific approach and techniques used in social skills training may vary depending on the individual's age, functioning level, and specific challenges. Here are some common strategies employed in autism social skills training:

DIRECT INSTRUCTION: This may include visual aids, role-playing exercises, or video modeling to teach specific social behaviors and rules.

SOCIAL STORIES: Short stories or narratives that describe social situations and appropriate behaviors.

VISUAL SUPPORTS: Items such as visual schedules, social scripts, or cue cards can be used to provide visual cues and reminders about appropriate social behaviors.

MODELING AND IMITATION: Therapists, teachers, or peers may demonstrate and model specific social skills to provide examples for individuals to learn from.

SOCIAL SKILLS GROUPS: These groups will play cooperative games, role-playing, and group discussions to facilitate social interaction and skill development.

PRACTICE AND REINFORCEMENT: Regular practice and reinforcement of social skills are crucial for skill acquisition and generalization.

GENERALIZATION AND MAINTENANCE: It's essential to generalize social skills in various environments. This involves helping individuals apply their learned social skills outside of the training setting

PEERs

The PEERs (Program for the Education and Enrichment of Relational Skills) is a social skills intervention program for adolescents and young adults with Autism Spectrum Disorder. It was developed at UCLA by Dr. Elizabeth Laugeson and is a world-renowned evidence-based social skills treatment. It provides a structured and supportive environment for individuals with ASD to develop and improve their social skills, helping them to better navigate social situations and improve their overall quality of life.

The PEERs program is based on social learning theory, which posts that social skills can be learned through observation, modeling, and reinforcement. The program is evidence-based, and research has shown it to be effective in improving social skills and reducing social anxiety in individuals with ASD.

Trained professionals facilitate the program, typically involving 6 to 10 individuals with Autism who meet weekly for 14 to 16 weeks.

In addition to the group sessions, participants are encouraged to practice their newly acquired social skills outside the program with family, friends, and peers. This is done through homework assignments and activities designed to reinforce the skills learned in the group sessions.

Cognitive Behavior Therapy (CBT)

CBT is a form of psychotherapy that can help with difficulties in social interaction, communication, and repetitive behaviors. CBT aims to help improve a person's overall functioning and well-being by teaching them new coping skills and strategies to manage their thoughts, emotions, and behaviors.

CBT is a talk therapy approach that focuses on identifying and changing negative thoughts, feelings, and behaviors contributing to mental health issues or other challenges. CBT can be adapted to address various problems, including anxiety, depression, obsessive-compulsive behaviors, and social skills deficits.

For younger children, CBT may be adapted to include more play-based interventions and visual aids to help them understand and engage with the therapy. For older children and adolescents, CBT may consist of more direct discussion and problem-solving around specific issues they face.

CBT MAY INVOLVE A VARIETY OF TECHNIQUES

COGNITIVE RESTRUCTURING

This involves helping identify and challenge negative or unhelpful thoughts contributing to their difficulties and replacing them with more positive and constructive thoughts.

EXPOSURE THERAPY

This involves gradually exposing the individual to what triggers their anxiety or distress in a controlled and supportive environment.

BEHAVIORAL SKILLS TRAINING

This involves teaching the individual new coping skills and behaviors that can help them manage their thoughts, emotions, and behaviors more positively and constructively.

PROBLEM-SOLVING

This involves helping individuals identify and solve problems in their lives by teaching them new skills and strategies for decision-making, planning, and problem-solving.

CBT is based on the idea that our thoughts, feelings, and behaviors are connected and that changing one can have a positive impact on the others

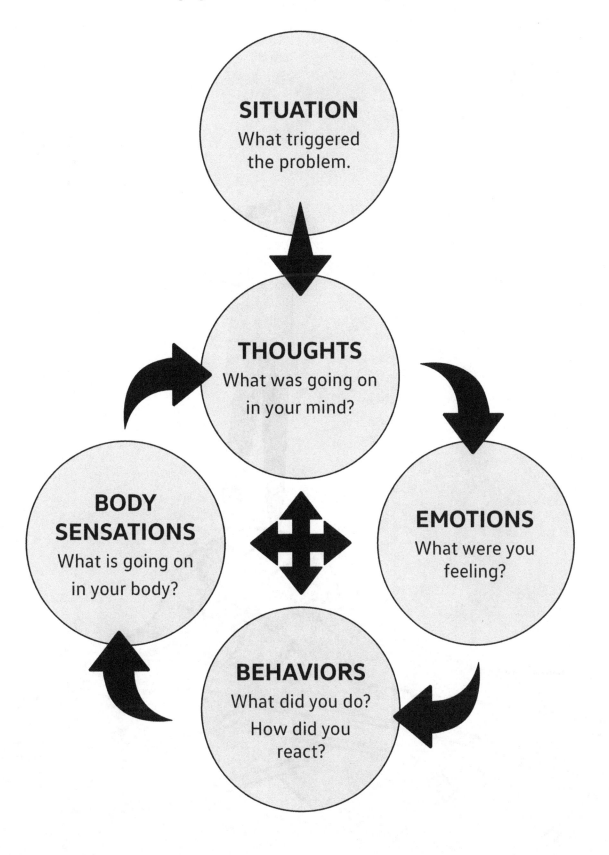

THE SECRET AUTISM ROADMAP

Complementary and Alternative Therapies

"It is a time to focus on abilities, not disabilities."

— Jason Shawndale Steen

Complementary and Alternative Therapies for Autism (CAM)

CAM treatments are defined as being outside the standard or mainstream treatments. There are only a few established treatments. CAM therapies include many practices and products not considered part of conventional medicine.

It's important to note that while some CAM therapies may be helpful for some individuals, there is limited scientific evidence to support their effectiveness. Additionally, some CAM therapies may be harmful or interact with other medications, so it's essential to consult with a healthcare professional before trying any CAM therapies.

Here are some examples of CAM therapies that you may consider:

- **DIETARY INTERVENTIONS:** Eliminating certain foods or adding supplements.

- **MIND-BODY THERAPIES:** Such as meditation, or yoga.

- **SENSORY-BASED THERAPIES:** These include music therapy, art therapy, and sensory integration therapy.

- **HERBAL REMEDIES:** Herbal remedies that may improve sleep or anxiety.

Mind-body Therapies

Several types of mind-body therapies may be helpful. It is important to note that the effectiveness of these mind-body therapies may vary depending on the individual needs and preferences of each person. Here are a few examples:

YOGA: A mind-body practice that combines physical postures, breathing exercises, and meditation. Promote relaxation, and improve sensory processing and regulation.

TAI CHI: Tai Chi is a martial art that involves slow, gentle movements and deep breathing. It can help improve balance, coordination, and sensory processing.

SENSORY INTEGRATION THERAPY: A type of occupational therapy that focuses on helping individuals with sensory processing difficulties to respond to sensory information.

MEDITATION: A practice that involves focusing one's attention on a specific object or thought to achieve mental calm and clarity. It can help improve self-awareness.

BIOFEEDBACK: A technique that uses electronic monitoring equipment to measure physiological responses such as heart rate, blood pressure, and muscle tension.

Therapeutic Horseback Riding

Therapeutic horseback riding is a type of recreational therapy that uses horses to provide physical, emotional, and sensory benefits to individuals with autism. Therapeutic riding helps individuals with autism relax and develop muscle tone, coordination, confidence, and well-being.

DEVELOPING AN EMOTIONAL BOND

Children experience physical contact with horses rather than verbal communication. They brush them, hug them, and pat them. By learning to care for the horse, they associate their care with feelings and construct an emotional bridge. This bond can also lead to social and communication skill production with other people in his life.

COGNITIVE AND LANGUAGE SKILLS DEVELOPMENT

Children that have difficulty comprehending standard directions. By engaging in equine therapy, children learn to follow paths through a fun activity that makes taking directions easier to grasp and remember. They also give the horse direction, giving them more opportunities to communicate, and the child is naturally motivated to move.

SENSORY BENEFITS

Balance and spatial orientation are experienced through the vestibular sense organs. These are located inside the inner ear and are stimulated through direction change, incline, and speed. Riding a horse helps liven these sensory preceptors, which helps make therapy exciting and motivates your child to continue to be engaged.

Overall, hippo therapy can provide a unique and beneficial therapeutic experience. It can improve physical, social, and emotional skills in a fun and engaging way and may help the child build confidence and self-esteem.

Emotional Support Animals (ESAs)

Emotional support animals can benefit individuals with autism. Here are some potential benefits:

REDUCED ANXIETY

ESAs can help reduce anxiety and stress levels in individuals with autism. Animals, such as dogs and cats, can provide comfort and a calming presence, which can help individuals with autism feel more relaxed and at ease.

INCREASED SOCIAL INTERACTION

ESAs can also help increase social interaction for individuals with autism. Some animals, such as dogs, can serve as a social bridge, assisting individuals with autism to initiate and maintain social interactions with others.

IMPROVED COMMUNICATION

ESAs can also improve communication for individuals with autism. For example, suppose an individual with autism has difficulty expressing emotions. In that case, an animal may be able to pick up on their nonverbal cues and respond in a way that helps the individual feel understood.

INCREASED SENSORY INPUT

ESAs can also provide increased sensory input for individuals with autism. Touching or petting an animal can provide a calming sensory experience for individuals with autism and help them develop their sensory processing skills.

It's important to note that not all children may benefit from an emotional support animal, and it's essential to carefully consider whether an ESA is the right choice for the individual's needs.

Arts Therapy

Art therapy can benefit children by providing a nonverbal form of expression to help individuals communicate and process their emotions and experiences. People with autism often have difficulty expressing themselves verbally or understanding social cues. Art therapy can provide a safe and creative outlet for them to explore and communicate their thoughts and feelings.

Art therapy can also help individuals with autism develop their fine motor skills, which can be challenging for some individuals. Additionally, engaging in art therapy can improve attention span, focus, and concentration and provide a sense of relaxation and stress relief.

Overall, art therapy can be an effective therapeutic intervention for individuals with autism, as it allows them to express themselves comfortably and meaningfully while also promoting their social, emotional, and cognitive development.

Art and expressions of creativity help to forge a more profound understanding of people. Many people use their creative pursuits to grow closer to their peers, express their needs, or decipher their emotions.

DANCE   **DRAMA**   **VISUAL**   **MUSIC**

Recreational Therapy

Community-based sports and recreation programs can provide many benefits, including:

PHYSICAL FITNESS

Participating in sports and recreation activities can improve overall physical health and fitness. This can be especially important for individuals who may have sensory processing difficulties and be prone to a sedentary lifestyle.

SOCIAL SKILLS

Community-based sports and recreation programs can provide opportunities for individuals to practice their social skills in a structured environment. These programs can help individuals with autism develop friendships, learn appropriate social behaviors, and increase their confidence in social situations.

SENSE OF BELONGING

Participating in community-based sports and recreation programs can provide individuals with autism with a sense of belonging and connection to their community. This can be especially important for individuals with autism who may struggle with social isolation.

IMPROVED SELF-ESTEEM:

Participating in sports and recreation activities can provide individuals with a sense of accomplishment and improve their self-esteem. Success in sports and recreation activities can also improve confidence and willingness to take on new challenges.

STRESS REDUCTION

Sports and recreation activities can provide a fun and engaging way for individuals to reduce stress and improve their overall well-being. These programs can provide an outlet for stress and anxiety, leading to improved mental health.

Overall, community-based sports and recreation programs can benefit individuals. These programs can improve physical fitness, social skills, sense of belonging, self-esteem, and stress reduction.

Nutritional Therapy

Nutritional therapy aims to improve the nutritional status and overall health of individuals. This therapy is based on the idea that certain nutrients and dietary changes can positively impact the symptoms and behavior of autism.

There is limited scientific evidence to support the idea that specific diets can significantly improve symptoms of autism. While some individuals with autism may have food sensitivities or digestive issues that can be addressed through dietary changes, there is currently no diet that has been scientifically proven to treat the core symptoms of autism.

One diet that has been promoted is the gluten-free, casein-free (GFCF) diet, which eliminates wheat (gluten) and dairy (casein) products. However, there is limited scientific evidence to support the effectiveness of this diet, and many experts believe that the benefits of the GFCF diet are primarily anecdotal.

Nutritional therapy may involve a variety of techniques, including:

ELIMINATION DIETS
This involves eliminating certain foods or food groups, such as gluten, casein, sugar, or artificial preservatives, that may contribute to behaviors.

SUPPLEMENTATION
This involves adding specific vitamins, minerals, or other dietary supplements to the individual's diet to improve their nutritional status and address deficiencies.

DIET MODIFICATION
This involves changing the individual's diet to improve overall nutrition and address specific nutritional needs.

PROBIOTICS AND FERMENTED FOODS
This involves adding probiotics, such as yogurt or kefir, and fermented foods, such as sauerkraut or pickles, to the individual's diet to improve their health and address any gut-related issues.

Herbal Remedies

In general, the most-recommended CAM options for autism are for specific symptoms such as sleeplessness or anxiety, and they are the same CAM options that are recommended for anyone with these issues.

Specifically, they include:

MELATONIN
A hormone made by the pineal gland, is known to help treat insomnia.

MULTIVITAMINS/MINERALS
With a recommended daily allowance of nutrients can ensure proper nutrition for children with autism who are picky eaters.

MASSAGE THERAPY
A well-established and risk-free alternative for reducing anxiety and stress.

In addition to these conservative recommendations, some doctors and therapists also recommend:

FISH OIl
Supplements (omega-3 fatty acids) for hyperactivity

VITAMIN B12
For behavioral issues

PROBIOTICS
For gastrointestinal issues

These treatments may or may not be particularly effective for any individual; only a few studies have explored their efficacy, and all of the studies are quite small. Results are inconclusive. They are considered unlikely to do any harm and are not too expensive.

Neighborhood Clubs, Groups, or Sports

There are several neighborhood clubs, groups, and sports activities that can be beneficial for an autistic child. Here are some suggestions:

CLUBS OR GROUPS

Is your child interested in video games or chess? Find groups or clubs that share their interest.

MARTIAL ARTS

These activities promote self-discipline, focus, and physical coordination while providing a structured and predictable environment.

SCOUTS

Scouting organizations, such as Boy Scouts or Girl Scouts, often have programs that welcome children with autism. These groups provide opportunities for personal growth.

ARTS/MUSIC CLASSES

Look for local art studios, theater groups, or music schools that offer classes or workshops.

SOCIAL SKILLS GROUPS

Many communities have social skills groups or organizations that are tailored for children with autism. These groups focus on developing social interaction and play skills through structured activities and games.

SPORTS TEAMS

Some local little leagues, soccer, or swimming teams work with autistic children. Make sure there are proper supports in place.

Tips for preparing child for Neighborhood Clubs, Groups, or Sports

When considering any club or activity, it's crucial to assess the specific needs and interests of the autistic child and ensure you have proper support in place. Also, consult with professionals or therapists to properly prepare the child for the activity and prepare them for difficulties.

WORK WITH THE COACH

Contact the coach or sports program coordinator to discuss your child's needs. Share information about your child's strengths, challenges, and any specific accommodations they may require. Collaboration with the coach is crucial for creating an inclusive and supportive environment.

PROPER PREPARATION

Introduce the child to the sport. Let them watch videos or play the sport with parents, siblings, therapists, or friends at a park. Create a visual schedule or social story to help them understand what to expect during practices and games.

MAKE SURE THERE ARE SUPPORTS

Attend team practices and games. Volunteer as an assistant coach, or bring a therapist to act as an aide to support but encourage independence over time. Provide encouragement and positive reinforcement, such as rewards, for their efforts and achievements.

MONITOR PROGRESS AND ADJUST AS NEEDED

Regularly assess the child's experience and progress on the sports team. Communicate with the coach and make adjustments as necessary to ensure the child's needs are being met.

**THE SECRET
AUTISM ROADMAP**

_____

Therapy Tools and Resources

_____

"Autism is about finding a way to survive in an overwhelming, confusing world... It is about developing differently, in a different pace and with different leaps.

— *Author Unknown*

THE SECRET

The secret is autistic children are visual learners. Visuals play a crucial role in learning, communication, and emotional well-being. By utilizing visual supports, you can create an environment that caters to each individual's unique strengths and needs, leading to improved learning outcomes and overall quality of life.

ENHANCED COMMUNICATION

Visuals provide a concrete and consistent way to communicate information, which is highly beneficial for children with receptive and expressive language challenges. Visual cues help bridge the gap in communication and understanding.

VISUAL LEARNING STRENGTHS

Visual learners process and understand information better when it is presented visually. Visual aids, such as pictures, charts, and graphs, tap into this learning strength, making it easier for them to grasp concepts and instructions.

REDUCED ANXIETY BY OFFERING PREDICABILITY

Visuals can help reduce Anxiety and uncertainty by offering predictability and structure. Visual schedules, for instance, provide a clear outline of the day's activities, assisting children to know what to expect and what is coming next, improving transitions.

IMPROVED TASK COMPLETION

Checklists and step-by-step guides break down complex tasks into manageable steps, making it easier for autistic children to follow and complete activities independently.

INCREASED INDEPENDENCE

By using visuals, children can better understand and follow routines and instructions on their own.

BEDTIME ROUTINES

SCHEDULES

SOCIAL STORIES

CHECKLISTS

Visual Schedules

Visual schedules are a tool to help manage daily routines and activities. It is a schedule that is presented visually, using pictures, illustrations, or symbols to represent different tasks and events.

Some Autistic children struggle with predicting their schedules. They miss social clues, which a visual schedule helps them understand and follow verbal instructions, assists with transitions, and reduces anxiety. Visual schedules help with morning routines, evening routines, and school schedules and routines.

VISUAL SCHEDULES
PROMOTES STRUCTURE AND PREDICTABILITY

VISUAL SCHEDULES
IMPROVES UNDERSTANDING OF ABSTRACT CONCEPTS LIKE TIME AND SEQUENCING

VISUAL SCHEDULES
FACILITATES INDEPENDENCE BY PROVIDING CLEAR UNDERSTANDING

VISUAL SCHEDULES
INCREASES MOTIVATION WITH VISUALS AND REWARDS

VISUAL SCHEDULES
IMPROVES TIME MANAGEMENT WITH A CLEAR TIMELINE

VISUAL SCHEDULES
REDUCES CHALLENGING BEHAVIORS BY PROVIDING A CLEAR UNDERSTANDING

VISUAL SCHEDULES
ENHANCES EXECUTIVE FUNCTIONING SUCH AS PLANNING AND ORGANIZING

VISUAL SCHEDULES
SUPPORTS TRANSITIONS AND REDUCES ANXIETY

VISUAL SCHEDULES
INCREASES FLEXIBILITY BY ALLOWING THEM TO SEE SCHEDULES IN ADVANCE

VISUAL SCHEDULES
INCREASES GENERALIZED SKILLS TO ENVIRONMENTS OR SITUATIONS

Social Stories

Social or preparation stories are a great teaching tool. They help prepare those who struggle with social understanding, navigating new situations, and understanding social norms. They are short, descriptive stories that describe a situation or scenario, including the perspectives of others, and guide appropriate behavior and responses.

The stories often use simple language, pictures, and visual supports to make the information easier to understand. They can be used to teach a wide range of social skills, such as making eye contact, sharing, going places, taking turns, understanding personal space, and managing emotions.

DEVELOPING SOCIAL STORIES

Social stories can be used to help with navigating everyday events or new and unusual social situations and interactions.

Here are some steps to creating a social story:

- **IDENTIFY THE SITUATION:** The first step is to identify the situation the individual is struggling with.

- **DEFINE THE KEY ELEMENTS:** Once you have identified the situation, define the key factors that will be included in the story.

- **DETERMINE THE PERSPECTIVE:** Decide on the view that the story will be told from.

- **WRITE THE STORY:** Using simple language and clear illustrations or pictures, write the story.

- **REVIEW AND REVISE:** Once the story is written, review it and make any necessary revisions.

- **IMPLEMENT AND REINFORCE:** Use the social story with the individual in a supportive environment, and reinforce positive behaviors.

- **REMEMBER:** A quick, poorly written social story is always much better than no social story.

Going to the Dentist

Bee Social Skills

Sometimes you have to go to the dentist. The dentist will clean your teeth and make sure they are healthy.

The dentist will have a big chair for you to sit in and will have equipment so they can take pictures of your teeth and clean them.

Then the dentist will ask me to open your mouth so they can clean and check your teeth.

Social or preparation stories help the child anticipate and prepare for social events or activities and reduces anxiety and frustration.

You brush your teeth.

We go to dentist and sit in the waiting room.

You sit in the dentist chair.

Dentist says hello.

Then the dentist looks in your mouth and cleans your teeth.

Then we go home.

Routine Charts

A routine chart is a visual tool to help children follow a routine. It is a type of visual schedule that represents a sequence of activities or events. The chart can include pictures, symbols, or words describing each routine step.

Routine charts can help children understand daily routines, such as getting dressed, brushing teeth, or completing homework, as well as more complex routines, such as preparing for a trip or an outing. They can provide structure, predictability, and a sense, which can help reduce stress and anxiety.

Routine charts can be used with other strategies, such as reinforcement, positive reinforcement, or prompts, to help individuals with autism understand and complete the routine. They can also be modified as needed to accommodate routine changes or address new challenges.

Daily Routine Chart

☀ Morning

- ✔ Wake Up
- ✔ Eat Breakfast
- ✔ Wash Up
- Brush Teeth
- Get Dressed
- Comb Hair
- Clean Up
- Go to School

☾ Evening

- Eat Dinner
- Take a Bath
- Brush Teeth
- Put on Pajamas
- Clean Up
- Go to the Toilet
- Read a Book
- Go to Sleep

★	★	★				★	★	★		
MON	TUES	WED	THUR	FRI		MON	TUES	WED	THUR	FRI

Calm Down Techniques

Calming down techniques can be helpful for individuals who experience stress, anxiety, or sensory overload. Here are some commonly used calm-down methods:

 **DEEP BREATHING:** Encourage the individual to take slow, deep breaths and to focus on the breath going in and out. This can help to slow the heart rate and relax the body.

 **PROGRESSIVE MUSCLE RELAXATION:** Teach the individual to tensing and then relaxing each muscle group in the body, starting with the feet and moving up to the head.

 **SENSORY INPUT:** Provide the individual with sensory input they find calming, such as a weighted blanket, a relaxing bath, a calming scent, or soft music.

 **VISUALIZATION:** Encourage the individual to visualize a calming scene, such as a beach, a forest, or a meadow, and to focus on the sights, sounds, and sensations of the scene.

 **MINDFULNESS:** Teach the individual to be present at the moment and to focus on their senses and surroundings. This can help to reduce stress and anxiety.

 **PHYSICAL ACTIVITY:** Encourage the individual to engage in physical activity, such as stretching, yoga, or walking, to release tension and promote relaxation.

 **SENSORY ROOMS:** A sensory room may provide a calming environment for individuals with autism, with soft lighting, calming sounds, and calming textures.

Calm Down Kits

A calm down kit can help calm down a child and help them control their emotions and behavior in times of stress or anxiety. Each chiild is different, so what works for one individual may not work for another, and it may take some trial and error to find the right calming techniques for each individual.

SENSORY TOYS
stress balls or
fidget spinners

COMFORT ITEMS
stuffed animal or blanket,
can provide security

VISUAL AIDS
Books or Social Stories
can help children relax

NOISE-CANCELLING HEADPHONES
helps block out
overwhelming sounds

JOURNALS OR COLORING BOOK
coloring or writing can
be a soothing activity

RELAXATION TECHNIQUES
breathing exercises or
relaxation techniques

Emotional Cards

Emotional cards help individuals recognize, understand, and express emotions. They typically consist of cards with pictures or illustrations of emotions like happiness, sadness, anger, fear, and surprise.

Emotional cards can help individuals who may have difficulty recognizing and expressing emotions to develop their emotional awareness and vocabulary. For example, a child may be shown a happy face picture and asked to identify the emotion being expressed. The individual may then be asked to describe the exact feeling through body language, facial expressions, or gestures.

Emotional cards are often incorporated into therapies and interventions, such as social skills training, cognitive behavioral therapy, and developmental interventions. They can be a helpful tool for individuals to develop their emotional awareness and understanding of emotions in others, which can lead to improved social interactions and communication.

How Are You Feeling?

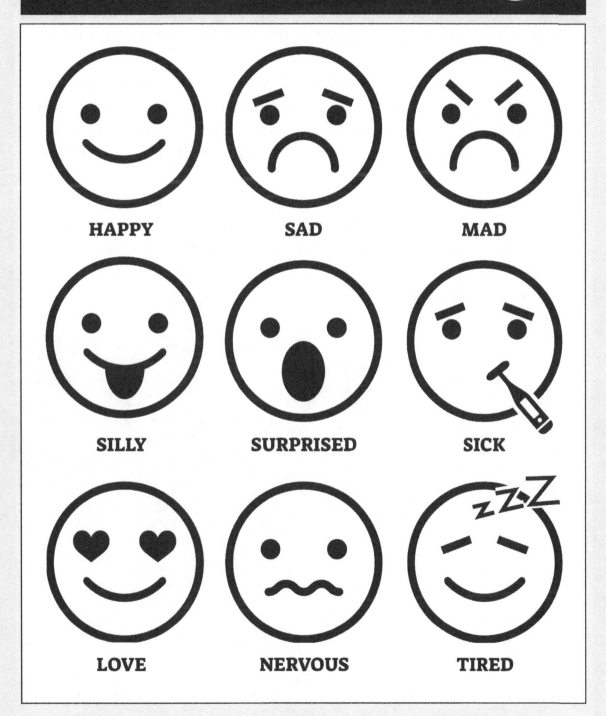

HAPPY   SAD   MAD

SILLY   SURPRISED   SICK

LOVE   NERVOUS   TIRED

Picture Exchange Communication System (PECS)

PECS stands for Picture Exchange Communication System. PECS is a method of alternative communication commonly used with individuals with autism or other communication difficulties.

PECS uses pictures or symbols to communicate wants, needs, and ideas. The individual is taught to exchange a picture card in exchange for the desired item or action. Individuals becoming more skilled with the system may learn to combine pictures to create more complex messages. The system can also be phased out as their communication improves.

The PECS system is based on the idea that individuals with autism are often more comfortable and motivated to communicate using visual images rather than traditional verbal communication. With consistent practice and reinforcement, individuals with autism can use PECS to communicate more effectively and confidently in various settings.

Data Tracking Forms

Data collection forms can vary depending on their purpose and the type of information being collected. Still, they generally include a set of questions or prompts that are used to guide observations and assessments. These forms can be completed by a variety of individuals, such as parents, caregivers, teachers, or healthcare professionals.

Data collection forms can be used to track progress over time, identify patterns and trends in behavior, and inform treatment decisions. For example, a data collection form may be used to track the frequency and intensity of a child's meltdowns over weeks or months. This information can then be used to develop a behavior plan or intervention to help manage the child's behavior.

Overall, data collection forms are a helpful tool for gathering and analyzing information and can help individuals with autism and their caregivers make informed decisions about treatment and support.

Behavior Frequency Data

Date: March 12-16

Name: David H.	Recorder: Stephanie K.					
Skill	M	T	W	TH	F	Total
Makes appropriate eye contact when speaking to partner.	0	2	1	0	1	4
Shifts gaze to what partner is looking at.	0	0	0	1	0	1
Self monitors volume of voice when speaking.	1	0	2	0	0	3
Meltdowns during transitions.	3	0	1	1	0	5

Reward Cards

Reward cards are used to promote positive behavior and encourage social skills. Reward cards can have a visual component, with pictures or symbols representing the rewards that can be earned. The cards may also have a tracking component, where progress toward earning rewards can be tracked and monitored.

The rewards on these cards are tailored to the individual's interests and needs and can include various items or activities, such as toys, books, snacks, or social interactions. For example, a child may be rewarded for completing tasks such as brushing their teeth or getting dressed independently. As that behavior becomes ingrained, the length of receiving a reward can grow, perhaps after five days of brushing their teeth or getting dressed separately, allowing the new skill to become a constant behavior not requiring rewards.

These cards can be used in various settings, such as at home, school, or therapy sessions. Reward cards are great at helping individuals understand and follow the rules, learn new skills, and improve behaviors. They can also provide a visual reminder of the rewards that can be earned, which can help to motivate and engage children.

Reward cards are an excellent tool for promoting positive behavior and social skills in individuals.

YOU CAN DO IT!

Achieve your Behavioral Contract for five days and win.
Initial each day as you achieve your goal.

1 | 2 | 3 | 4 | 5

RACE TO TEN

Complete ten days of achieving your
Behavioral Contract goal(s) and win.

Color each day as you
achieve your goal.

DAILY GOAL

Name: _____

Date: _____

Goals: _____

_____

☺ ☺ ☹

Notes: _____

_____

Signature: _____

Additional Tools and Resources

TIMERS

Timers can be used as a helpful too for a variety of purposes:

- Timers can also be used as a visual reminder of how long an activity will go on and helps develop a better understanding of what is expected of them, reinforcing positive behaviors. This helps reduce anxiety and increase predictability.
- Assists in breaking down activities into stages.
- Is used as a visual aid to reinforce positive behaviors.

TALLY COUNTERS

Tally counters can be a valuable tool to track behaviors or events and make progress toward their goals.

NOISE-REDUCTION HEADPHONES

Noise-reduction headphones help manage sensory sensitivity.

- Excessive noise levels can trigger anxiety and stress.
- Provides a sense of control over their sensory experiences.

AAC DEVICE

An augmentative and alternative communication device is a tablet or laptop that helps someone with a speech or language impairment to communicate.

SENSORY TOYS

Sensory toys regulate a person's sensory input and provide a calming and soothing effect. Sensory toys include fidget spinners, squishy balls, chew toys, tactile toys, and visual stimulators (such as light-up toys or toys with moving parts).

FINE MOTOR GAMES

Many fine motor games and activities can benefit children by improving hand-eye coordination, finger strength, and agility. Here are some examples:

- **PLAYDOUGH:** Roll, shape, and manipulate the dough.
- **BEADING AND LACING:** Beading and lacing activities involve threading tiny beads or objects onto a string or a pipe cleaner.
- **CUTTING AND PASTING:** Cutting and pasting activities will also improve visual perception and spatial awareness.
- **BUILDING BLOCKS:** Building blocks can help improve spatial awareness, hand-eye coordination, and problem-solving skills.
- **PUZZLES:** These can be a fun and challenging way to improve problem-solving and spatial awareness.
- **DRAWING AND COLORING:** Children can experiment with different drawing tools, such as crayons, markers, and colored pencils.
- **TWEEZERS AND TONGS:** Can be used in fine motor activities, such as picking up small objects or sorting materials.

GROSS MOTOR SKILLS

Gross motor skills involve muscle groups, such as running, jumping, and throwing. Toys that promote gross motor development can help improve strength and coordination. Here are some examples of gross motor toys:

- **BALANCE BOARDS:** Balance boards are a toy that can help improve balance and coordination.
- **TRAMPOLINES:** Can provide a fun and engaging way to improve gross motor skills, including coordination, balance, and strength.
- **SCOOTERS:** Require the use of both legs and can help improve coordination and balance.
- **LARGE BALLS:** Large balls can also provide sensory input through tactile stimulation.
- **OBSTACLE COURSES:** Obstacle courses can be created using a variety of toys and equipment, such as cones, tunnels, and balance beams.

THE SECRET
AUTISM ROADMAP

Home Program

"Navigating the special needs system can feel like trying to solve a puzzle with missing pieces."

— Author Unknown

THE SECRET

The secret is the home program is the most essential element in your child's therapy programs. It is the hub of all your child's programs. It is critical because it ensures an individualized working approach is applied to all activities. When there are behavioral issues, it ensures that interventions are quickly and appropriately applied. A home program should be convenient and accessible and provide a safe, conducive area for learning and promoting progress.

A good home program offers flexibility in implementation and adjusting the program as needed. It allows for frequent and consistent practice, crucial for skill acquisition and retention. It is important to note that a home program should be developed in collaboration with professionals, such as a BCBA ABA supervisor. They can provide guidance, set goals, and suggest appropriate strategies and activities.

Understanding what skills and behaviors need to be worked on when requesting services.

When requesting services or requesting services to be continued, explaining what skills and behaviors are being worked is extremely helpful. The following pages list common skills and behaviors your child should work on or achieve. You can use the list to compile a list of skills and behaviors you are working on or will be working on.

If your current therapy or program isn't capable of achieving those skills, you will need to find a program that will be able to reach those skills.

OUTINGS
- Family Trips
- Doctor/Dentist Visit
- Grocery Store
- Restaurants

COMMUNITY PARTICIPATION
- Community Events
- Community Activities
- Safety Skills

SCHOOL
- Before School, Breaks, and Lunch
- Class Room Education
- Clubs, Sports, or Activities

THE HOME PROGRAM
The home program should be monitoring and overseeing all programs preferably with the assistance of an outside specialist like an ABA BCBA manager.

HOME THERAPY PROGRAMS
- ABA Program
- Speech
- OT

DAILY LIVING
- Managing Time and Money
- Self Care
- Leisure Time
- Chores

OUTSIDE SCHOOLING ACTIVITIES
- Homework
- Tutoring

Home Therapy Programs

The child's home setting is the best area for receiving early intervention. The child is more comfortable in the home, and behaviors will more quickly be applied to life at home. Many parents can get started with early intervention therapies by reading, watching videos, or attending classes online or in person. Parents can also receive training from a trained therapist and then take over and continue those therapies as they feel more comfortable. Even if parents choose to work with a therapy program outside the home, they can also learn to provide therapy for their child between therapy sessions, thus building their skills while lowering the cost of therapy.

EARLY INTERVENTION

Play Therapy	Floortime/DIR Model	Early Start Denver Model (ESDM)
Relationship Development Intervention (RDI)		Pivotal Response Treatment (PRT)

Many early intervention techniques use Child-Centered Play where the parents/therapist encourage the child to engage in pretend play using toys and props to encourage shared attention, communication, bonding, flexible thinking, problem-solving, and skill-building.

APPLIED BEHAVIOR ANALYSIS (ABA)

ABA is referred to as the gold standard of autism therapy, mainly because therapists set very specific, measurable goals and often succeed in teaching those skills. The process can be fairly simple and intuitive:

1. Choose the skill you want to teach (for example: brush your teeth).

2. Break the skill down into simple steps (find your toothbrush, wet it, etc.).

3. Go over the steps explaining and demonstrating them.

4. If they do a good job, praise and reward them.

5 If they struggle, go back to step 1 and try to include visual references or social stories to help your child understand the process.

6. Once your child is successful with the first step, teach the second step.

SENSORY INTEGRATION THERAPY

A home is a great place to create a sensory-friendly environment. Simple items can provide sensory experiences and help the child engage in sensory activities tailored to their sensory needs.

SWING SET: promotes relaxation and body awareness.

LARGE INFLATABLE BALLS: for play, bouncing, rolling, or sitting on to improve balance and coordination.

TACTILE SENSORY MATERIALS: Sand or water play kits to stimulate touch.

FIDGET TOYS: small handheld objects with different textures, shapes, or movements that can be squeezed, pulled, or twisted.

CHEW TOYS: chewing necklaces or toys that provide a safe outlet for oral sensory needs.

VISUAL SENSORY MATERIALS: light projectors, lava lamps, or lights that provide visual stimulation.

VISUAL TIMERS: Visual cues or displays to help anticipate time.

SENSORY BINS: containers filled with materials like rice, beans, or sand to explore and engage their senses.

NOISE-CANCELING HEADPHONES: reduce or block out external noises.

BALANCE BOARDS: Boards or discs that encourage balance and body control.

SCENTED MATERIALS: Essential oils to promote relaxation or focus.

SPEECH THERAPY

Many aspects of speech therapy can be provided with little training.

1. Encourage Communication
2. Read Together
3. Sing and Rhyme Together
4. Play Language Games
5. Play Interactive Games
6. Use Visual Supports
7. Provide Social Interactions

OCCUPATIONAL THERAPY

There are ways parents can support their child's occupational therapy goals at home:

1. Incorporate sensory activities into your child's daily routine.
2. Offer activities that promote the development of fine motor skills.
3. Engage your child in play activities that target specific occupational therapy goals.

The Importance of Home Therapy Goals

A common phrase is that each person is different, but the truth is that most autistic children have the same deficits that need to be worked on. As your home and school programs are being developed, use the checklists in this section to review and ensure you cover the common concerns.

Home therapy goals should focus on developing independence, maximizing potential, and improving one's life through goal-setting. These goals will help the children grow up and become active participants in society, embracing their strengths and overcoming life's constant challenges.

- Developing independence fosters a sense of empowerment, self-confidence, and autonomy, leading to increased overall well-being and quality of life.

- Maximizing potential is another crucial aspect of finding unique strengths, abilities, and interests. Individuals can reach their full potential and explore their passions by identifying and nurturing these strengths.

- Improving one's life is a fundamental objective and encompasses various aspects, including physical, emotional, social, and cognitive well-being.

HOME THERAPY GOALS

Home goals can be broken down into sub categories. A comprehensive home program should address all areas of need.

BEHAVIOR MANAGEMENT SKILLS

PLAY AND LEISURE SKILLS

COMMUNICATION SKILLS

PERSONAL SAFETY SKILLS

DAILY LIVING SKILLS

PRE-ACADEMIC SKILLS

EMOTIONAL INTELLIGENCE SKILLS

SELF-ADVOCACY SKILLS

EXECUTIVE FUNCTIONING SKILLS

SELF-HELP SKILLS

FINE MOTOR SKILLS

SELF-MONITORING SKILLS

FLEXIBILITY SKILLS

SELF-REGULATION
AND COPING SKILLS

GENERALIZATION OF SKILLS

SENSORY INTEGRATION SKILLS

GROSS MOTOR SKILLS

SOCIAL SKILLS

ORGANIZATION SKILLS

TASK COMPLETION SKILLS

PARENT TRAINING AND SUPPORT

VISUAL PERCEPTION SKILLS

BEHAVIOR MANAGEMENT SKILLS

Behavior management skills are essential to learn and develop appropriate behaviors.

- [ ] Following instructions.
- [ ] Waiting their turn.
- [ ] Using appropriate greetings.
- [ ] Sharing toys and materials.
- [ ] Using manners.
- [ ] Accepting "no" as a response.
- [ ] Using problem-solving skills.
- [ ] Using coping strategies when upset.
- [ ] Taking turns in conversations.
- [ ] Asking for help when needed.
- [ ] Engaging in cooperative play.
- [ ] Managing personal space.
- [ ] Accepting feedback or criticism.
- [ ] Accepting changes in routines.
- [ ] Transitioning between activities smoothly.
- [ ] Using appropriate voice volume.
- [ ] Using appropriate eye contact during conversations.
- [ ] Respecting personal boundaries.
- [ ] Resolving conflicts peacefully.
- [ ] Identifying and expressing emotions.
- [ ] Recognizing social cues and nonverbal communication.
- [ ] Engaging in reciprocal conversations.

- [ ] Following social rules and norms.
- [ ] Responding appropriately to praise and compliments.
- [ ] Using problem-solving skills to resolve conflicts.
- [ ] Understanding and respecting personal differences.
- [ ] Recognizing and managing personal emotions.
- [ ] Accepting constructive feedback.
- [ ] Demonstrating empathy and understanding others' perspectives.
- [ ] Negotiating and compromising in social situations.
- [ ] Recognizing and managing stress or anxiety.
- [ ] Respecting personal boundaries.
- [ ] Respecting personal belongings of others.
- [ ] Recognizing and understanding body language & facial expressions.
- [ ] Accepting redirection.
- [ ] Demonstrating flexibility in adapting to changes.
- [ ] Using personal hygiene skills.
- [ ] Recognizing and avoiding potentially dangerous situations.

COMMUNICATION SKILLS

Communication skills involve listening, speaking, and observing through face-to-face interactions, phone conversations, and digital communications.

- [ ] Making and maintaining eye contact during interactions.
- [ ] Sharing attention and focus with others.
- [ ] Engaging in back and forth conversations.
- [ ] Expressing needs or wants verbally or through gestures.
- [ ] Making observations or sharing information.
- [ ] Carrying out verbal or visual instructions.
- [ ] Seeking information or clarification through questioning.
- [ ] Responding to questions with relevant information.
- [ ] Identifying and verbalizing feelings and emotions.
- [ ] Starting conversations with others.
- [ ] Staying on topic during conversations off.
- [ ] Greeting others and responding to greetings.
- [ ] Using gestures, facial expressions, or body language to convey meaning.
- [ ] Using words or gestures to describe objects, people, or events.
- [ ] Sharing personal experiences or recounting past events.
- [ ] Expressing positive feedback.
- [ ] Using communication skills to work through conflict.
- [ ] Engaging in discussions to find mutually agreeable solutions.
- [ ] Engaging in forming relationships.
- [ ] Understanding and responding to others' feelings.
- [ ] Understanding and using humor in social interactions.
- [ ] Taking turns and contributing ideas.
- [ ] Adjusting voice volume and tone for different situations.
- [ ] Providing or asking for clarification when unclear.
- [ ] Paying attention and responding during conversations.
- [ ] Interpreting phrases or expressions with non-literal meaning.
- [ ] Making and continuing phone conversations.
- [ ] Using communication skills to text or email.

DAILY LIVING SKILLS

Daily living skills promote independence and functional abilities.

- [ ] Brushing teeth, washing hands, and grooming tasks.
- [ ] Putting on and taking off clothes, fastening buttons or zippers.
- [ ] Using utensils, drinking from a cup, and self-feeding.
- [ ] Simple meal preparation tasks.
- [ ] Safely operating kitchen appliances.
- [ ] Putting away toys and cleaning.
- [ ] Straightening bedding and arranging pillows.
- [ ] Sorting and folding clothes.
- [ ] Operating the TV or other electronic devices.
- [ ] Recognizing and counting coins, making simple purchases.
- [ ] Understanding and following a daily schedule.
- [ ] Using a visual checklist to complete tasks.
- [ ] Learning to navigate and use public transportation.
- [ ] Understanding road signs, pedestrian safety, and rules.
- [ ] Making a shopping list and finding items in the store.

- [ ] Understanding and practicing emergency responses.
- [ ] Properly using public restroom hygiene.
- [ ] Sorting and arranging personal items.
- [ ] Basic phone and computer skills.
- [ ] Understanding and using a schedule or planner.
- [ ] Understanding appropriate behavior in public places.
- [ ] Learning to take medication with supervision.
- [ ] Understanding basic first aid.
- [ ] Basic household chores such as Dusting, sweeping, and vacuuming.
- [ ] Establishing morning and bedtime activities.
- [ ] Breaking down tasks to achieve them.
- [ ] Understanding money and budgeting.
- [ ] Expressing needs and asking for help.
- [ ] Setting goals and carrying out instructions.

EMOTIONAL INTELLIGENCE

Emotional intelligence refers to the ability to recognize, understand, and manage emotions in oneself and others.

- [ ] Identifying emotions.
- [ ] Expressing emotions.
- [ ] Understanding facial expressions.
- [ ] Recognizing body language.
- [ ] Understanding and sharing the feelings of others.
- [ ] Being able to see situations from another person's point of view.
- [ ] Paying attention and responding appropriately during conversations.
- [ ] Recognizing one's own emotions, strengths, and challenges.
- [ ] Developing strategies to manage and regulate one's own emotions.
- [ ] Learning healthy ways to cope with challenging emotions.
- [ ] Recognizing and managing emotional responses.
- [ ] Developing skills to solve social problems and conflicts.
- [ ] Being open to new ideas, and adapting to changes.
- [ ] Developing the ability to bounce back from setbacks.
- [ ] Believing in oneself and one's abilities.

- [ ] Identifying situations or events that may lead to heightened emotions or stress.
- [ ] Setting goals, staying focused, and maintaining motivation.
- [ ] Understanding nonverbal cues to navigate social interactions.
- [ ] Developing and nurturing friendships and other social connections.
- [ ] Expressing one's needs and wants.
- [ ] Recognizing and managing stress.
- [ ] Recognizing and managing anxiety.
- [ ] Being able to adapt emotions based on different situations.
- [ ] Identifying and appreciating one's own unique strengths and abilities.
- [ ] Understanding the impact of actions on others.
- [ ] Expressing appreciation for others.
- [ ] Practicing being present in the moment.
- [ ] Learning to resolve conflicts in a peaceful and constructive manner.
- [ ] Recognizing and managing anger.

EXECUTIVE FUNCTIONING SKILLS

Executive functioning skills involve various cognitive processes that help individuals plan, organize, problem-solve, and regulate their behavior.

☐ Planning and allocating time for different activities and tasks.

☐ Starting tasks independently without excessive delay or procrastination.

☐ Developing systems to keep belongings and information in order.

☐ Identifying and ranking tasks based on importance or urgency.

☐ Creating strategies and steps to reach short-term and long-term goals.

☐ Breaking down complex tasks into smaller, manageable steps.

☐ Adapting to changes in routines, plans, or expectations.

☐ Analyzing problems and generating solutions with effective strategies.

☐ Assessing one's own performance, progress, and behavior.

☐ Reflecting on actions, decisions, and outcomes to learn from experiences.

☐ Holding and manipulating information in mind for short periods.

☐ Sustaining attention on relevant tasks and filtering out distractions.

☐ Following through on tasks until they are finished.

☐ Resisting immediate impulses or urges and thinking before acting.

☐ Shifting thoughts, strategies, or perspectives when faced with new or changing situations.

☐ Thinking about one's own thinking processes and strategies.

☐ Managing emotions, behavior, and impulses in various situations.

☐ Evaluating options, considering consequences, and making choices.

☐ Stopping or inhibiting automatic responses or behaviors when necessary.

☐ Estimating the time required to complete tasks accurately.

☐ Transitioning between different tasks or activities efficiently.

☐ Understanding and adhering to rules and expectations.

☐ Regulating emotions, behavior, and impulses in challenging situations.

☐ Anticipating future needs, events, or challenges and preparing for them.

☐ Assessing one's strengths, weaknesses, and areas for improvement.

☐ Paying close attention to specific details and avoiding mistakes.

☐ Recognizing and managing emotions in oneself and others.

FINE MOTOR SKILLS

Fine motor skills involve coordinating small muscles in the hands and fingers, enabling precise movements and control.

- [ ] Using the thumb and index finger to pick up small objects.
- [ ] Cutting along lines or shapes with scissors.
- [ ] Practicing letter formation and improving handwriting skills.
- [ ] Staying within the lines and using different coloring techniques.
- [ ] Following lines or shapes with a pencil or marker.
- [ ] Buttoning and unbuttoning clothes.
- [ ] Zipping and unzipping zippers.
- [ ] Tying shoelaces.
- [ ] Holding and using a fork, spoon, or knife during meals.
- [ ] Pouring liquids from a pitcher.
- [ ] Opening and closing containers.
- [ ] Using tongs or tweezers to pick up small objects.
- [ ] Stringing beads or pasta onto a string.
- [ ] Threading a needle and basic sewing skills.
- [ ] Folding paper into specific shapes.
- [ ] Manipulating small objects or toys with precision.
- [ ] Turning pages in a book or magazine.

- [ ] Using a hole puncher to create holes in paper.
- [ ] Snapping or fastening snaps or buttons on clothing.
- [ ] Using a key to unlock and lock a door or padlock.
- [ ] Building with blocks or constructing with Legos.
- [ ] Playing with small manipulative toys like puzzles or building sets.
- [ ] Using a computer mouse or touchscreen device.
- [ ] Operating buttons, switches, or knobs on electronic devices.
- [ ] Playing musical instruments that require finger coordination.
- [ ] Squeezing and using hand strengtheners or stress balls.
- [ ] Tearing paper into strips.
- [ ] Rolling, squeezing, or shaping playdough or clay.
- [ ] Using a spoon to scoop and transfer objects from containers.
- [ ] Using a ruler or measuring tape to measure objects.
- [ ] Threading shoelaces.
- [ ] Turning doorknobs or handles.

FLEXIBILITY AND ADAPTABILITY SKILLS

Flexibility and adaptability skills are essential to effectively navigate changes, transitions, and new situations.

- ☐ Handling changes in routines or schedules without becoming upset.
- ☐ Trying new foods or accepting changes in meal options.
- ☐ Being open to different play ideas and incorporating them into routines.
- ☐ Accepting changes in plans or unexpected events.
- ☐ Switching focus between different topics or tasks when necessary.
- ☐ Adjusting to new social situations or meeting new people.
- ☐ Coping with changes in sensory input or sensory-rich environments.
- ☐ Being open to trying new activities, hobbies, or interests.
- ☐ Accepting alterations in the sequence or order of activities or steps in a task.
- ☐ Responding appropriately to changes in rules or expectations.
- ☐ Shifting from preferred activities to less preferred ones without resistance.
- ☐ Recognizing and adapting to changes in peer dynamics or group play.
- ☐ Being open to new strategies or approaches when problem-solving.
- ☐ Accepting changes in the daily or weekly schedule.

- ☐ Adapting to new classroom or educational settings.
- ☐ Adjusting the level of task difficulty or complexity based on abilities.
- ☐ Coping with unexpected interruptions or disruptions in routines.
- ☐ Adapting to changes in the physical environment or sleep routines.
- ☐ Adjusting communication style or language based on the needs.
- ☐ Recognizing and accepting changes in social rules or expectations in different contexts.
- ☐ Adjusting to changes in transportation methods or travel routines.
- ☐ Coping with changes in weather or seasonal transitions.
- ☐ Recognizing and adapting to changes in technology or electronic devices.
- ☐ Being open to accepting help or support from others when needed.
- ☐ Adapting to changes in clothing choices or preferences.
- ☐ Being open to modifications or adaptations in learning materials.
- ☐ Adjusting to changes in family routines or dynamics.

GENERALIZATION OF SKILLS

Generalizing skills involves applying learned skills and knowledge in various settings, with different people, and across different situations.

- [ ] Generalizing social skills.
- [ ] Applying communication skills with different communication partners.
- [ ] Generalizing self-help skills
- [ ] Transferring academic skills to real-life situations.
- [ ] Applying problem-solving strategies to different challenges and scenarios.
- [ ] Generalizing play skills to different play settings and with different toys.
- [ ] Transferring organization skills to different contexts.
- [ ] Generalizing fine motor skills to various activities.
- [ ] Applying safety skills in different environments.
- [ ] Transferring money skills to different stores or situations.
- [ ] Generalizing daily living skills to different settings.
- [ ] Applying time management skills to various schedules and routines.
- [ ] Transferring problem-solving skills to different academic subjects.
- [ ] Generalizing social skills to interactions with peers, or family members.
- [ ] Applying coping skills in different stressful or challenging situations.

- [ ] Generalizing community skills to different locations.
- [ ] Transferring computer skills to different software or applications.
- [ ] Generalizing organizational skills to different belongings and materials.
- [ ] Applying emotional regulation strategies in various emotional situations.
- [ ] Generalizing pre-academic skills to different contexts.
- [ ] Transferring cooking or meal prep skills to different recipes.
- [ ] Generalizing problem-solving strategies to real-life situations.
- [ ] Applying decision-making skills to different choices and situations.
- [ ] Generalizing gross motor skills to different physical activities.
- [ ] Transferring technology skills to different devices.
- [ ] Applying self-advocacy skills in different social settings.
- [ ] Transferring behavior management strategies to different settings.
- [ ] Generalizing problem-solving skills to real-life challenges and obstacles.

GROSS MOTOR SKILLS

Gross motor skills involve the coordination and control of large muscles and movements of the body.

- ☐ Walking independently and maintaining a steady pace.
- ☐ Running and jogging with coordination.
- ☐ Jumping with two feet together.
- ☐ Hopping on one foot.
- ☐ Skipping.
- ☐ Galloping.
- ☐ Climbing stairs with alternating feet.
- ☐ Walking up and down a ramp.
- ☐ Kicking a ball with accuracy.
- ☐ Throwing and catching a ball.
- ☐ Riding a tricycle or bicycle.
- ☐ Balancing on one foot.
- ☐ Standing on tiptoes.
- ☐ Jumping off a small height and landing safely.
- ☐ Performing simple dance movements or rhythmic exercises.
- ☐ Playing interactive games involving jumping, hopping, or running.
- ☐ Participating in organized sports activities (e.g., soccer, basketball).
- ☐ Swimming and water movements.
- ☐ Playing on playground equipment.
- ☐ Climbing and balancing on a climbing frame or rock wall.

- ☐ Participating in obstacle courses or agility training.
- ☐ Engaging in exercises that promote core muscle strength.
- ☐ Participating in martial arts or martial arts-inspired movements.
- ☐ Engaging in jumping jacks or other aerobic exercises.
- ☐ Playing with large exercise balls and engaging in ball-related activities.
- ☐ Engaging in relay races or team-based physical activities.
- ☐ Practicing coordination skills through activities like throwing and catching.
- ☐ Balancing and walking on a balance beam or line.
- ☐ Practicing different forms of jumping, such as hurdles or skipping ropes.
- ☐ Engaging in rhythmic activities with music, such as clapping or marching.
- ☐ Participating in group movements.
- ☐ Engaging in trampoline activities with supervision and precautions.
- ☐ Practicing kicking and hitting targets.
- ☐ Engaging in activities that promote spatial awareness.
- ☐ Participating in team activities that involve coordination and cooperation.

ORGANIZATION SKILLS

Organizational skills promote independence, time management, and overall efficiency in daily activities.

- [ ] Keeping personal belongings in designated places.
- [ ] Creating and following a daily routine or schedule.
- [ ] Organizing and categorizing toys or materials on type, color, or size.
- [ ] Using a calendar or planner to keep track of dates and appointments.
- [ ] Sorting and organizing clothes by type or season.
- [ ] Labeling drawers or containers for easy identification.
- [ ] Making a checklist or visual schedule to guide through activities.
- [ ] Establishing a system for organizing schoolwork or assignments.
- [ ] Setting up a designated study area with necessary supplies and materials.
- [ ] Planning and organizing personal care tasks for grooming routines.
- [ ] Using a timer or alarm to manage time and stay on schedule.
- [ ] Breaking down tasks or projects into smaller, manageable steps.
- [ ] Developing a system for managing and organizing files or documents.
- [ ] Creating a visual or written checklist for morning or bedtime routines.

- [ ] Setting goals and creating a plan to achieve them.
- [ ] Implementing strategies to organize personal belongings during travel.
- [ ] Using a whiteboard to keep track of reminders or to-do lists.
- [ ] Developing a system for organizing and managing personal finances.
- [ ] Creating and maintaining a chore chart or responsibilities list.
- [ ] Implementing strategies to keep track of and manage passwords.
- [ ] Organizing and maintaining a calendar of activities or social events.
- [ ] Using visual prompts or reminders to assist with transitions.
- [ ] Utilizing a visual or written schedule to plan and prepare for trips.
- [ ] Creating a system for organizing and storing art supplies or materials.
- [ ] Establishing a system for keeping track of important phone numbers.
- [ ] Using a visual or written schedule to plan for special events or holidays.
- [ ] Establishing a consistent system for organizing and storing sports gear.

PARENT TRAINING AND SUPPORT

Parent training and support play a crucial role.

- [ ] Understanding autism spectrum disorder (ASD) and its characteristics.
- [ ] Learning about evidence-based interventions and therapies.
- [ ] Implementing strategies for effective communication with your child.
- [ ] Building a positive and supportive relationship with their child.
- [ ] Understanding and managing challenging behaviors.
- [ ] Developing strategies for promoting social skills development.
- [ ] Creating a structured and predictable environment at home.
- [ ] Implementing visual supports and schedules to enhance communication.
- [ ] Supporting your child's sensory needs and providing sensory strategies.
- [ ] Promoting independence and self-help skills.
- [ ] Advocating for your child's educational rights and services.
- [ ] Supporting your child's participation in hobbies and interests.
- [ ] Fostering positive sibling relationships and providing support to siblings.
- [ ] Promoting play skills and engagement with peers.
- [ ] Addressing sleep difficulties and establishing a bedtime routine.
- [ ] Encouraging and supporting the development of motor skills.
- [ ] Enhancing parental self-care and stress management.
- [ ] Navigating the transition to adulthood and planning for the future.
- [ ] Addressing feeding difficulties and promoting healthy eating habits.
- [ ] Establishing a supportive network of other parents and support groups.
- [ ] Utilizing technology and assistive devices to support their child's needs.
- [ ] Developing strategies for successful inclusion in community activities.
- [ ] Managing and supporting challenging transitions in daily routines.
- [ ] Addressing and supporting the unique learning style of their child.
- [ ] Understanding and implementing behavior management techniques.
- [ ] Learning about available resources and services in their community.
- [ ] Promoting effective social communication skills, such as initiating and maintaining conversations.
- [ ] Building resilience and coping skills.

PARENT TRAINING BEHAVIORAL STRATEGIES

Behavior management is an important aspect of supporting children with autism

☐ Using positive rewards to encourage desired behaviors.

☐ Using visual supports to provide a predictable structure.

☐ Implementing a system where tokens or points are earned for positive behavior and can be exchanged for rewards.

☐ Allowing the child to make choices within structured options to promote independence.

☐ Using personalized stories to teach appropriate behaviors and social expectations.

☐ Communicating expectations by showing a preferred activity or reward after completing a non-preferred task.

☐ Using timers to indicate the duration of an activity or transition.

☐ Providing visual prompts or cues to support appropriate behavior.

☐ Breaking down complex tasks into smaller steps.

☐ Teaching alternative communication.

☐ Modifying the environment or situation to prevent challenging behaviors before they occur.

☐ Teaching the child to track and evaluate their own behavior.

☐ Providing verbal or physical praise to reinforce positive behavior.

☐ Identifying the function or purpose of challenging behaviors to develop targeted interventions.

☐ Implementing sensory breaks or offering sensory supports to address sensory needs.

☐ Teaching and practicing appropriate social skills through modeling and role-playing.

☐ Pairing the child with peers who can model appropriate behavior.

☐ Encouraging peers to support and reinforce positive behaviors in the child with autism.

☐ Using videos to demonstrate desired behaviors.

☐ Providing opportunities for the child to engage in preferred social activities.

☐ Include sensory activities or breaks throughout the day to help regulate the child's sensory system.

PLAY AND LEISURE SKILLS

Developing play and leisure skills is crucial for children as it promotes social interaction, imagination, creativity, and overall enjoyment.

- [ ] Engaging in imaginative play with dolls or action figures.
- [ ] Participating in turn-taking games and activities with peers or siblings.
- [ ] Playing board games and following game rules.
- [ ] Participating in cooking or baking activities with supervision.
- [ ] Engaging in role-play activities (e.g., playing doctor or firefighter).
- [ ] Engaging in sensory play with playdough, sand, or water.
- [ ] Creating and designing artwork through drawing, painting, or crafts.
- [ ] Playing with musical instruments or engaging in music-related activities.
- [ ] Engaging in physical play, such as tag, hide-and-seek, or catch.
- [ ] Playing with puzzles or engaging in problem-solving games.
- [ ] Engaging in building and engineering activities, such as LEGO.
- [ ] Engaging in outdoor play, such as swinging or playing in a sandbox.
- [ ] Participating in pretend play with dress-up costumes or props.
- [ ] Engaging in sensory art activities, such as finger painting or sensory bins.

- [ ] Playing with musical toys or doing singing and dancing activities.
- [ ] Engaging in construction play with tools or building sets.
- [ ] Playing with dolls or action figures, engaging in storytelling.
- [ ] Engaging in social play activities, such as tea parties or playing house.
- [ ] Participating in sports activities, such as kicking a ball or swimming.
- [ ] Engaging in rhythm and movement activities, such as dancing or using rhythm instruments.
- [ ] Playing with interactive toys or games that encourage cause-and-effect relationships.
- [ ] Engaging in sensory activities with bubbles, balloons, or sensory bottles.
- [ ] Playing with animals or engaging in pet-related activities.
- [ ] Engaging in water play activities, such as playing with water toys or having a water balloon fight.
- [ ] Engaging in gardening activities.
- [ ] Participating in storytelling activities, such as creating and telling their own stories.

PERSONAL SAFETY SKILLS

Developing personal safety skills is essential for children to ensure their well-being and security in various situations.

- [ ] Recognizing and responding to their own name.
- [ ] Learning and practicing personal identification information, such as their full name and address.
- [ ] Identifying and using appropriate greetings and responses in social interactions.
- [ ] Understanding personal boundaries and respecting others' personal space.
- [ ] Identifying and understanding different warnings, alarms, or safety signs and symbols.
- [ ] Learning and practicing emergency procedures, such as dialing emergency numbers.
- [ ] Understanding and following basic road safety rules, such as looking both ways before crossing.
- [ ] Practicing stranger awareness and understanding safe interactions.
- [ ] Understanding and responding appropriately to different social cues, such as body language or tone.
- [ ] Practicing basic first aid skills, such as applying bandages.
- [ ] Understanding and following rules for safe play and participation in sports activities.
- [ ] Understanding and following rules for using public transportation.
- [ ] Learning and practicing appropriate ways to ask for help when needed.
- [ ] Understanding and responding to different types of warnings or alarms.
- [ ] Practicing problem-solving skills to navigate challenging situations.
- [ ] Following kitchen safety rules, such as using utensils and appliances safely.
- [ ] Practicing appropriate use of technology and internet safety.
- [ ] Following rules for playground safety.
- [ ] Learning and practicing personal finance skills, such as handling money.
- [ ] Recognizing and understanding safe behavior around animals.
- [ ] Learning and practicing water safety skills, such as swimming with supervision and using life jackets.
- [ ] Recognizing and avoiding potential hazards in the environment, such as sharp objects or slippery surfaces.
- [ ] Practicing appropriate behavior in public restrooms and understanding privacy boundaries.
- [ ] Practicing appropriate behavior during mealtime, such as chewing food properly and avoiding choking.

PRE-ACADEMIC SKILLS

Developing pre-academic skills lays the foundation for future learning and academic success.

- [ ] Identifying and naming uppercase and lowercase letters.
- [ ] Associating letters with their sounds.
- [ ] Recognizing and manipulating sounds in words, such as rhyming.
- [ ] Recognizing ones own name.
- [ ] Identifying and naming numbers from 1 to 10 in sequence.
- [ ] Identifying and naming shapes.
- [ ] Identifying and naming colors.
- [ ] Categorizing objects based on attributes like color, shape, or size.
- [ ] Finding and matching objects or pictures that are the same.
- [ ] Recognizing and creating simple patterns using colors or shapes.
- [ ] Organizing and representing data using basic graphs or charts.
- [ ] Understanding the concepts of size, length, and weight.
- [ ] Arranging objects in order based on size, length, or quantity.
- [ ] Understanding and arranging objects or events in chronological order.
- [ ] Developing fine motor skills for writing, such as tracing shapes.
- [ ] Developing hand-eye coordination and letter formation skills.
- [ ] Cutting along lines and shapes.
- [ ] Engaging in fine motor skills, such as stringing beads or using tweezers.
- [ ] Identifying differences and similarities in shapes, patterns, or objects.
- [ ] Understanding the left-to-right directionality of reading and writing.
- [ ] Following multiple-step directions and responding to auditory cues.
- [ ] Developing the ability to stay focused on a task.
- [ ] Engaging in activities that encourage logical thinking.
- [ ] Developing the ability to analyze information and make decisions.
- [ ] Using prepositions, such as in, on, or under, or behind.
- [ ] Using words that describe location, such as next to, beside, or between.
- [ ] Identifying and describing different types of weather and seasons.
- [ ] Understanding and using a calendar to identify days and months.
- [ ] Recognizing sight words.
- [ ] Writing their name or simple words.
- [ ] Basic math concepts.
- [ ] Identifying and counting coins, understanding their value.

SELF-ADVOCACY SKILLS

Developing self-advocacy skills empowers children to express their needs, preferences, and rights effectively.

- [ ] Recognizing and communicating their likes and dislikes.
- [ ] Requesting accommodations or modifications in school settings.
- [ ] Expressing emotions and feelings.
- [ ] Maintaining conversations with peers and adults.
- [ ] Asking for clarification or repetition when instructions are unclear.
- [ ] Setting personal goals and working towards achieving them.
- [ ] Seeking help or support when needed.
- [ ] Making choices independently, such as selecting activities or food options.
- [ ] Respecting personal boundaries and the boundaries of others.
- [ ] Assertively expressing opinions or preferences in a respectful manner.
- [ ] Participating in decision-making processes that affect them.
- [ ] Negotiating and compromising in social interactions or conflicts.
- [ ] Recognizing and addressing bullying or discriminatory behavior.
- [ ] Understanding and advocating for their rights and responsibilities.
- [ ] Seeking opportunities for additional support or resources.

- [ ] Identifying and using appropriate strategies for self-regulation and emotional management.
- [ ] Requesting breaks or sensory supports when feeling overwhelmed.
- [ ] Building self-esteem through positive self-talk and affirmations.
- [ ] Self-monitoring and self-evaluating their progress or performance.
- [ ] Understanding and communicating their learning preferences or styles.
- [ ] Asking for clarification or additional information during academic tasks.
- [ ] Seeking feedback from teachers or peers to improve their work.
- [ ] Explaining their disability to others in a positive and informative manner.
- [ ] Use assistive technologies or tools that enhance their independence.
- [ ] Reflecting on their strengths and areas for improvement.
- [ ] Problem-solving skills to overcome challenges or obstacles.
- [ ] Self-advocating for modifications or accommodations in employment settings.
- [ ] Celebrating their achievements and successes with others.

SELF-HELP SKILLS

Developing self-help skills is essential for children to promote independence and daily living skills.

- [ ] Dressing independently, zipping, buttoning, and tying shoelaces.
- [ ] Using the toilet independently, including proper hygiene practices.
- [ ] Combing hair and brushing teeth properly.
- [ ] Taking a shower or bath independently.
- [ ] Getting dressed appropriately for different weather conditions.
- [ ] Applying sunscreen.
- [ ] Using utensils to eat meals.
- [ ] Opening and closing lunch boxes, snack bags, or food containers.
- [ ] Pouring drinks into cups or glasses without spilling.
- [ ] Using a napkin or tissue to clean up spills or wipe their nose.
- [ ] Packing and unpacking their backpack or school bag.
- [ ] Putting away toys, books, or other belongings in their places.
- [ ] Making their bed and keeping their bedroom tidy.
- [ ] Using a calendar or planner to keep track of important dates and events.
- [ ] Using technology devices, such as computers or tablets.

- [ ] Taking care of pets, such as feeding, grooming, or walking.
- [ ] Using a telephone to make simple calls or send messages.
- [ ] Using a microwave or toaster safely to prepare simple snacks.
- [ ] Safely using basic household tools, such as scissors or kitchen utensils.
- [ ] Using appropriate table manners and following mealtime etiquette.
- [ ] Operating home appliances, such as a washing machine or dishwasher.
- [ ] Handling money, and making basic purchases.
- [ ] Preparing a simple meal or snack.
- [ ] Cleaning up spills or messes promptly.
- [ ] Using public transportation, such as understanding schedules, buying tickets, and following travel routes.
- [ ] Following a basic daily routine or schedule independently.
- [ ] Engaging in self-care activities, such as applying lotion, or deodorant.
- [ ] Managing time and completing tasks within given deadlines.
- [ ] Safely crossing the street using crosswalks and obeying signals.

SELF-MONITORING SKILLS

Self-monitoring is an essential skill that allows children to become more aware of their own behavior, emotions, and performance.

- [ ] Recognizing and identifying their own emotions.
- [ ] Noticing changes in their body, such as heart rate or breathing patterns, during different situations.
- [ ] Monitoring their own progress towards achieving personal goals.
- [ ] Monitoring their attention and focus during activities or tasks.
- [ ] Identifying when they need a break.
- [ ] Recognizing signs of frustration or anger and calming strategies.
- [ ] Monitoring their energy levels and recognizing when they need to rest.
- [ ] Noticing when overwhelmed and implementing coping strategies.
- [ ] Tracking and reflecting on their own academic or learning progress.
- [ ] Monitoring their interactions and recognizing their impacts.
- [ ] Identifying situations or triggers that may cause sensory overload.
- [ ] Noticing and reflecting on their own strengths and areas for improvement.
- [ ] Monitoring their own organization and time management skills.
- [ ] Recognizing when they need assistance and asking for help.
- [ ] Tracking their own daily routines and schedules.
- [ ] Monitoring their own personal hygiene habits, such as brushing teeth or washing hands.
- [ ] Recognizing when they need to use relaxation techniques.
- [ ] Tracking their own eating habits and recognizing when they are full.
- [ ] Monitoring their own sleep patterns and recognizing the importance of a consistent sleep routine.
- [ ] Identifying and reflecting on their own social skills and interactions.
- [ ] Recognizing their own personal boundaries and respecting others.
- [ ] Monitoring their own use of technology and screen time.
- [ ] Tracking and reflecting on their own problem-solving abilities.
- [ ] Monitoring their safety awareness and recognizing potential risks.
- [ ] Recognizing when they need to adjust their strategies or approaches in academic or social situations.
- [ ] Tracking and reflecting on their own leisure and recreational activities.
- [ ] Tracking and reflecting on their own independence and self-help skills.

SELF-REGULATION AND COPING SKILLS

Developing self-regulation and coping skills is crucial for children to effectively manage their emotions, behavior, and sensory needs.

- [ ] Using a visual or written schedule to anticipate changes in routine.
- [ ] Taking sensory breaks or engaging in sensory activities as a coping skill.
- [ ] Practicing mindfulness techniques to stay focused and present.
- [ ] Using positive self-talk and/or self-affirmations to build self-esteem.
- [ ] Engaging in movement activities to reduce stress, such a swinging, running, or jumping on a trampoline.
- [ ] Deep breathing exercises to promote relaxation and calmness.
- [ ] Using a designated quiet space for relaxation and self-regulation.
- [ ] Implementing a structured daily routine to provide predictability.
- [ ] Use problem-solving skills to find solutions to challenging situations.
- [ ] Use a sensory toolkit or tools like a fidget toy, stress ball, or other tactile object to self-soothe.
- [ ] Practicing self-calming strategies, such as muscle relaxation.
- [ ] Expressing emotions through art, writing, or other creative outlets.
- [ ] Engaging in calming sensory activities, such as listening to music or using calming scents.
- [ ] Manage frustration using strategies like counting or taking a break.
- [ ] Using sensory grounding techniques, such as focusing on the five senses, to stay present and calm.
- [ ] Using social stories or visual supports to navigate social situations.
- [ ] Developing relaxation techniques, such as progressive muscle relaxation.
- [ ] Recognizing different emotions and using coping strategies for each.
- [ ] Developing a system for self-reward to accomplish goals or tasks.
- [ ] Practicing social skills, such as active listening, to navigate interactions.
- [ ] Engaging in hobbies or special interests as a way to relax.
- [ ] Using problem-solving steps, such as brainstorming solutions and evaluating options.
- [ ] Developing and using a social support network, including friends, family, or support groups.
- [ ] Practicing self-advocacy skills to express needs and seek support.
- [ ] Using practical communication skills to express feelings and needs.

SENSORY INTEGRATION

Sensory integration focuses on helping individuals process sensory information and develop appropriate responses to sensory stimuli.

- ☐ Engaging in deep-pressure activities, such as using a weighted blanket or receiving a firm hug.

- ☐ Exploring different textures through sensory bins or touch-based activities.

- ☐ Engaging in water activities, such as water play or splashing water.

- ☐ Using sensory fidget toys to provide tactile stimulation and promote focus.

- ☐ Playing with sensory balls of various sizes and textures.

- ☐ Participating in messy play activities, such as finger painting.

- ☐ Exploring auditory experiences, such as listening to calming music.

- ☐ Engaging in proprioceptive activities, such as jumping on a trampoline.

- ☐ Playing with sensory sand or kinetic sand to promote tactile exploration.

- ☐ Engaging in swinging activities to provide vestibular stimulation.

- ☐ Participating in pretend play activities, such as dressing up or role-playing.

- ☐ Using noise-canceling headphones to reduce auditory sensitivity.

- ☐ Engaging in movement-based activities, such as yoga or dancing.

- ☐ Experiment with visual stimuli, such as colorful lights or lava lamps.

- ☐ Playing with different sensory textures, such as slime or putty.

- ☐ Using a sensory swing or hammock to provide calming vestibular input.

- ☐ Engaging in deep breathing exercises to promote self-regulation.

- ☐ Exploring different tastes and food textures through mealtime activities.

- ☐ Engaging in sensory walks or nature exploration to stimulate the senses.

- ☐ Engaging in calming sensory activities, such as blowing bubbles

- ☐ Playing with sensory tubes or sensory bottles to promote visual tracking.

- ☐ Engaging in sensory art activities, such as making textured collages or using textured materials for painting.

- ☐ Using sensory chew toys to address oral sensory needs.

- ☐ Engaging in balance activities, such as walking on a balance beam.

- ☐ Playing with sensory tubes filled with different materials, like rice or beans.

- ☐ Engaging in sensory-based science experiments, such as exploring states of matter or making sensory slime.

- ☐ Participating in sensory cooking or baking activities to explore different tastes, textures, and smells.

SOCIAL SKILLS

Developing social skills is crucial for children to effectively interact and communicate with others.

- [ ] Recognizing and making eye contact during conversations.
- [ ] Initiating greetings and farewells.
- [ ] Taking turns during conversations.
- [ ] Utilize active listening and responding appropriately.
- [ ] Asking for clarification.
- [ ] Sharing toys or materials with others.
- [ ] Responding to non-verbal cues, such as facial expressions or body language.
- [ ] Showing empathy and understanding others' feelings.
- [ ] Use social rules in different settings.
- [ ] Maintaining conversations on topics of interest to others.
- [ ] Respecting personal boundaries and other people's possessions.
- [ ] Participating in group activities.
- [ ] Recognizing and understanding social hierarchies or social roles.
- [ ] Resolving conflicts or disagreements peacefully and respectfully.
- [ ] Understanding and using appropriate greetings based on social context.
- [ ] Recognizing different perspectives or points of view.
- [ ] Recognizing and interpreting others' emotions through facial expressions and body language.
- [ ] Engaging in cooperative play.
- [ ] Understanding and following the rules of social etiquette.
- [ ] Recognizing social cues.
- [ ] Understanding and respecting diversity and cultural differences.
- [ ] Maintaining conversations with peers and adults.
- [ ] Demonstrating good sportsmanship during games or competitions.
- [ ] Showing appreciation and giving compliments to others.
- [ ] Recognizing different perspectives or points of view.
- [ ] Using appropriate social language and tone of voice in different contexts.
- [ ] Demonstrating appropriate behavior in public places, such as restaurants.
- [ ] Recognizing and understanding social norms in different environments.
- [ ] Recognizing and responding to social cues in online interactions.
- [ ] Using appropriate body language.
- [ ] Recognizing and understanding sarcasm in social interactions.

TASK COMPLETION SKILLS

Developing task-completion skills is vital for children to plan, organize, and complete tasks effectively.

- ☐ Breaking down tasks into smaller, more manageable steps.
- ☐ Setting goals and objectives for tasks.
- ☐ Creating a visual schedule or checklist to track task progress.
- ☐ Prioritizing tasks based on importance and urgency.
- ☐ Using timers or alarms to stay on track and manage time effectively.
- ☐ Following multi-step directions.
- ☐ Maintaining focus and attention on a given task.
- ☐ Identifying potential distractions and implementing strategies.
- ☐ Seeking assistance when encountering difficulties.
- ☐ Planning and organizing materials or resources needed for a task.
- ☐ Using visual supports or written prompts to guide task completion.
- ☐ Implementing strategies to manage frustration or setbacks.
- ☐ Monitoring progress and adjusting strategies as needed.
- ☐ Breaking down complex tasks into smaller, more manageable subtasks.
- ☐ Developing problem-solving skills to overcome obstacles or challenges.

- ☐ Using effective study strategies, such as creating flashcards.
- ☐ Practicing time management skills, such as estimating task duration.
- ☐ Seeking feedback and reflecting on task performance for improvement.
- ☐ Using organizational tools, such as planners or digital calendars.
- ☐ Implementing strategies to maintain a clean and organized workspace.
- ☐ Applying problem-solving techniques to identify alternative solutions.
- ☐ Developing self-monitoring skills to evaluate and adjust performance.
- ☐ Developing strategies to manage distractions and maintain focus.
- ☐ Practicing task initiation skills to start tasks independently.
- ☐ Seeking peer collaboration or assistance for group tasks.
- ☐ Using visual supports, such as graphic organizers, to organize ideas.
- ☐ Applying problem-solving strategies to overcome barriers or obstacles
- ☐ Developing strategies to prioritize and manage multiple tasks.
- ☐ Celebrating and acknowledging accomplishments upon completion.

VISUAL PERCEPTION SKILLS

Visual perception skills play a crucial role in a child's ability to interpret and understand visual information.

- [ ] Following the movement of objects with the eyes.
- [ ] Differentiating between similar objects or shapes.
- [ ] Remembering and recalling visual information.
- [ ] Recognizing incomplete or partially hidden images.
- [ ] Arranging objects or images in a specific order.
- [ ] Understanding the position and orientation of objects.
- [ ] Differentiating an object from its background.
- [ ] Identifying and tracking moving objects or changes in visual stimuli.
- [ ] Using visual cues and information to solve puzzles
- [ ] Methodically searching and examining a visual scene.
- [ ] Focusing and sustaining attention on visual stimuli.
- [ ] Coordinating visual information with motor actions.
- [ ] Completing or filling in missing parts of a visual image.
- [ ] Noticing details within a larger scene.

- [ ] Recognizing and understanding symmetry in patterns.
- [ ] Understanding spatial relationships.
- [ ] Making accurate judgments of size, distance, or quantity.
- [ ] Solving puzzles that require visual perception.
- [ ] Recognizing and creating patterns using visual stimuli.
- [ ] Locating specific objects or information within a display.
- [ ] Following a model and reproducing it visually.
- [ ] Identifying familiar objects or symbols even when they are partially obscured or distorted.
- [ ] Recognizing letters, numbers, or shapes in different fonts.
- [ ] Recalling and describing from memory.
- [ ] Differentiating between similar colors, or patterns.
- [ ] Understanding one's own body position in space.
- [ ] Comparing and understanding relative sizes of objects or images.

Breaking the Divide

It is vital to have a unified program of therapy. As your child enters the school system, new programs will be introduced using different terminology and techniques. This can be pretty confusing and frustrating for a young child, so having a unified program that follows working strategies is crucial.

Consistency and continuity are vital in promoting progress and optimal outcomes. When multiple professionals or caregivers support an individual, a unified program ensures everyone is on the same page and working towards common goals. By following strategies that have shown effectiveness, such as evidence-based interventions and best practices, the individual receives consistent support and reinforcement across different settings. This helps to establish routines, build upon learned skills, and minimize confusion or conflicting approaches, leading to improved learning and generalization of skills.

A unified program also enables effective data collection and progress monitoring. When everyone involved in the individual's care uses the same strategies and tracking progress consistently, gathering accurate data on the individual's development becomes more manageable. This data allows for informed decision-making, adjustments to interventions as needed, and the identification of areas where further support or modifications may be required.

Lastly and often, one of the most challenging elements is to create a unified program that fosters collaboration and communication among professionals, caregivers, and educators. By sharing a common framework and strategies, team members can effectively collaborate, exchange information, and align their efforts. This promotes a holistic and integrated approach to support the individual's needs, encourages sharing insights and experiences, and facilitates coordinated decision-making. Collaboration among professionals and caregivers ensures that the individual's goals and progress are consistently addressed across various environments, leading to a more comprehensive and cohesive support system.

In summary, a unified program facilitates collaboration among professionals and caregivers, leading to a more coordinated and comprehensive approach to support. By aligning efforts and building upon what has been proven to work, individuals can receive consistent and effective interventions that maximize their potential for growth and development.

Therapy Exhaustion

If an autistic child appears overworked and traumatized during therapy, it may be a sign that the therapy is not meeting their needs or is too intense.

Here are some steps that you can take to address this situation:

TALK TO THE THERAPIST
Discuss your concerns and seek their professional opinion on how to proceed.

ASSESS THE THERAPY GOALS
Review the therapy goals to ensure that they are appropriate and achievable.

REDUCE THE FREQUENCY OF THERAPY SESSIONS
Consider reducing the frequency of therapy sessions if the child is overworked.

SEEK ALTERNATIVE THERAPIES
Explore alternative therapies, such as play therapy or music therapy, which may be more suitable for the child's needs and abilities.

ADDRESS ANY UNDERLYING ISSUES
If the child is showing signs of trauma, it may be necessary to address any underlying issues, such as a traumatic event, abuse, or neglect.

CONSIDER THE CHILD'S WELL-BEING
Always prioritize the child's well-being and ensure that therapy is not causing harm or stress.

It's important to remember that therapy should always be supportive, positive, and respectful of the child's needs and abilities. If the therapy is causing harm or stress, reassessing and making changes may be necessary to ensure the child's well-being.

Therapy Isn't Working

If your child is not responding to therapy, it's important to consider the following steps:

- **REVIEW THE THERAPY PLAN**
Ensure that the therapy plan is appropriate for your child's individual needs and goals and that the therapist is qualified and experienced in working with children with autism.

- **CONSIDER A DIFFERENT TYPE OF THERAPY**
Different types of therapy, such as speech, occupational, and behavior therapy, may be more effective for some children.

- **FIND A NEW THERAPIST**
If your child is not progressing with the current therapist or agency, consider finding a new one who fits your child's needs better.

- **REASSESS THE DIAGNOSIS**
It's possible that the initial diagnosis was incorrect, or your child may have co-occurring conditions that need addressing. Consult with a specialist to reassess your child's needs.

- **TRY ALTERNATIVE APPROACHES**
In addition to traditional therapy, alternative, complementary therapies may be effective for some children.

- **SEEK ADDITIONAL SUPPORT**
Consider joining a support group for families of children or seeking additional resources and support from local organizations and advocacy groups.

Remember that every child is unique; what works for one child may not work for another. It's important to remain persistent, flexible, and open-minded in finding the proper support for your child.

THE SECRET
AUTISM ROADMAP

Special
Education Law

"Special education is not just about academic achievement; it's about empowering students to become self-determined, independent, and contributing members of society."

— Author Unknown

THE SECRET

The secret is that special education law is on your side, but it is very difficult to get enforced. School districts play fast and loose with special education law if not defiantly flaunting it, so it is crucial to understand your rights and what the law says, means, and implies.

Special education law protects the rights of students with disabilities and ensures they receive appropriate educational services. These laws are designed to guarantee that students with disabilities have equal access to education and receive an education tailored to their individual needs.

The most important of these laws is the Individuals with Disabilities Education Act. IDEA is a federal law that sets forth the rights and requirements for students with disabilities in the educational system. It mandates that eligible students receive a free appropriate public education in the least restrictive environment.

Under IDEA, students with disabilities are entitled to an individualized education program, a written document that outlines their specific educational goals and the services and support they will receive to achieve those goals. The IEP is developed through a collaborative process involving parents or guardians, teachers, and other relevant professionals.

Additionally, IDEA ensures procedural safeguards for students and their families, including the right to due process and the opportunity to resolve disputes through mediation or a formal hearing. In addition to these laws are the Americans with Disabilities Act (ADA) and Section 504 of the Rehabilitation Act. These laws aim to eliminate discrimination and ensure equal opportunities for individuals with disabilities in various aspects of life, including education.

The Elementary and Secondary Education Act (1965)

The ESEA of 1965 was enacted as part of President Lyndon B. Johnson's "War on Poverty" initiative to address the educational disparities between low-income and minority students and their more advantaged peers. The law aimed to ensure that all students, regardless of background, have access to quality education.

The main provisions are:

- Aims to enhance educational opportunities for low-achieving students.

- Developed measures to assess student progress and hold schools accountable.

- Promotes professional development opportunities for teachers and school leaders to enhance their knowledge and instructional practices.

- Emphasizes the involvement of parents and families in their child's education.

- Supports initiatives to maintain safe and drug-free learning environments, addressing violence, substance abuse, and school discipline policies.

Vocational Rehabilitation Act (1973)

The Vocational Rehabilitation Act of 1973, also known as the Rehabilitation Act, prohibits discrimination against individuals with disabilities. Section 504 of the Rehabilitation Act states that no qualified individual with a disability can be excluded from, denied access to, or subjected to discrimination under any program or activity that receives federal funding.

Key features are:

- Section 504 prohibits discrimination against individuals with disabilities.

- Entitles reasonable accommodations or modifications to enable individuals with disabilities to participate fully.

- Section 504 guarantees eligible students with disabilities the right to a free appropriate public education.

- Ensures that facilities, programs, and services are accessible to individuals with disabilities.

- Establishes procedures for handling complaints and grievances related to disability discrimination.

The Education Amendments Act (1974)

The Education Amendments Act amended several existing laws, including the Elementary and Secondary Education Act (ESEA) and the Higher Education Act (HEA) to address educational issues and promote equality and access to education.

Some of the notable provisions include:

- **TITLE IX:** Prohibits sex discrimination in educational programs and activities that receive federal financial assistance.

- **BILINGUAL EDUCATION:** Supports bilingual education programs for students with limited English proficiency.

- **IMPACT AID:** Provides federal funding to school districts to alleviate the financial burden on these districts and promote educational equity.

- **SPECIAL EDUCATION:** Emphasizes the rights of students with disabilities to receive a free appropriate public education (FAPE) and established safeguards and procedures to protect their rights.

- **PELL GRANTS:** The Act expanded the Pell Grant program aimed to increase access to post-secondary education for low-income students.

- **VOCATIONAL EDUCATION:** The Act supported developing and improving vocational education programs to prepare students for careers.

Education for All Handicapped Children Act (1975)

The EAHCA of 1975 marked the first comprehensive federal legislation addressing the educational rights of students with disabilities.

The key principles are:

- **FREE APPROPRIATE PUBLIC EDUCATION (FAPE):** Children with disabilities have the right to receive a free appropriate public education.

- **INDIVIDUALIZED EDUCATION PROGRAM (IEP):** Requires the development of an individualized education program (IEP) for each child with a disability.

- **LEAST RESTRICTIVE ENVIRONMENT (LRE):** Also known as PL 94-142 states that students with disabilities should be educated to the maximum extent possible alongside their non-disabled peers in the least restrictive environment.

- **PROCEDURAL SAFEGUARDS:** Established procedural safeguards to protect the rights of students and their families. These safeguards include provisions for parental involvement, the right to due process, and mechanisms for resolving disputes and conflicts.

The Education of the Handicapped Act Amendments of 1986

The EHAA expanded and refined several aspects of the original legislation to strengthen and improve the Act.

- Extended Age Range to 3 to 5 years, ensuring early intervention services.

- Specifically recognized autism and traumatic brain injury as an eligible disability.

- Includes individualized transition plans as part of the IEP process.

- Emphasizes the importance of assistive technology devices and services.

- Emphasis on parental involvement and participation in the educational decision-making process.

The 1990 reauthorization changed the law's name from EHA to the Individuals with Disabilities Education Act, or IDEA

Americans with Disabilities Act (1990)

The Americans with Disabilities Act (ADA) has significantly improved the lives of people with disabilities by breaking down barriers and promoting inclusivity in various aspects of society.

The ADA was signed into law in 1990. Its purpose is to protect the rights of individuals with disabilities and ensure equal opportunities for them in various aspects of life. The ADA is divided into five titles, each addressing different areas of public life to prevent discrimination against individuals with disabilities. Here's a brief overview of what each title covers:

- **TITLE I: EMPLOYMENT** - This title prohibits discrimination against qualified individuals with disabilities in the workplace, and it requires employers to provide reasonable accommodations to enable employees with disabilities to perform their job duties.

- **TITLE II: PUBLIC SERVICES** - Title II applies to state and local government entities, including public transportation, public schools, and other government services. It mandates that public services and programs be made accessible to individuals with disabilities.

- **TITLE III: PUBLIC ACCOMMODATIONS** - Title III covers places of public accommodation, such as restaurants, hotels, movie theaters, and other privately-owned businesses that are open to the public. It requires that these places be accessible to individuals with disabilities.

- **TITLE IV: TELECOMMUNICATION**s - This title focuses on the telephone and television access for individuals with hearing and speech disabilities, aiming to ensure equal access to telecommunication services.

- **TITLE V: MISCELLANEOUS PROVISIONS** - Title V includes various provisions, including the relationship of the ADA to other laws, its impact on insurance providers, and the application of the law to specific situations.

Individuals with Disabilities Education Act

In 1990 the law's name from Education for All Handicapped Children Act (EHA was changed to the Individuals with Disabilities Education Act (IDEA).

1997 REAUTHORIZATION OF THE IDEA

It strengthened and expanded the rights and services provided to students with disabilities and their families. It aimed to improve educational outcomes and ensure that students with disabilities receive appropriate support and services to succeed in school and beyond.

2004 IDEA IMPROVEMENT ACT

It strengthens the rights of students with disabilities, improves educational outcomes, enhances teacher qualifications, and promotes early intervention strategies.

- **INCREASED ACCOUNTABILITY:** Introduced requirements for states to develop and implement performance goals and indicators to improve educational outcomes for students with disabilities.

- **HIGHLY QUALIFIED TEACHERS:** Special education teachers must be highly qualified and demonstrate expertise in the subject areas they teach.

- **EARLY INTERVENING SERVICES:** Provide early intervention services to students struggling academically but not yet identified with a disability.

- **RESPONSE TO INTERVENTION (RTI):** RTI involves providing targeted interventions and monitoring student progress to determine if additional support or evaluation for special education eligibility is needed.

- **ALIGNMENT WITH NO CHILD LEFT BEHIND:** The reauthorization of IDEA in 2004 aimed to align the law more closely with the goals and requirements of the No Child Left Behind Act (NCLB).

- **DISCIPLINE:** The IDEA Improvement Act clarified disciplinary procedures for students with disabilities. It ensures that disciplinary actions are not based on a student's disability. The reauthorization also provided guidelines for alternative educational settings for students with disabilities who are disciplined.

No Child Left Behind Act (2001)

NCLB was a federal education law in the United States that was enacted in 2001. It aimed to improve the quality of education and accountability in schools, particularly in relation to student performance and achievement.

The key aspects are:

- **ACCOUNTABILITY AND STANDARDS:** It required states to establish academic standards and develop annual assessments to measure student proficiency in core subjects, such as reading and math.

- **ADEQUATE YEARLY PROGRESS (AYP):** Schools were required to demonstrate yearly improvement in student test scores to ensure that all students would reach proficiency within a set timeframe.

- **HIGHLY QUALIFIED TEACHERS:** All teachers in core academic subjects must be highly qualified, meaning they have obtained the necessary academic credentials and demonstrated subject matter expertise in their teaching areas.

- **SCHOOL AND DISTRICT ACCOUNTABILITY:** It established consequences for schools that consistently failed to meet AYP targets, including the implementation of improvement plans, the provision of supplemental services, and the possibility of restructuring or takeover.

- **SCHOOL CHOICE AND SUPPLEMENTAL SERVICES:** Students from low-income families were allowed to transfer to higher-performing schools within their district. Schools failing to meet AYP had to offer supplemental

- **FOCUS ON CLOSING ACHIEVEMENT GAPS:** Schools were required to report and address disparities in achievement and implement strategies to improve outcomes for all student subgroups.

The No Child Left Behind Act aimed to increase transparency, accountability, and educational outcomes by setting clear standards, measuring student progress, and implementing consequences for underperforming schools. While it brought attention to educational disparities, it also received criticism for its emphasis on standardized testing and its unintended consequences on curriculum and instruction. The Every Student Succeeds Act (ESSA) later replaced the law in 2015.

Mental Health Parity and Addiction Equity Act (2008)

The Mental Health Parity and Addiction Equity Act (MHPAEA) is a federal law enacted in 2008 in the United States. The primary objective of this act is to ensure that health insurance coverage for mental health and substance use disorder (SUD) services is on par with coverage for medical and surgical services. In essence, it seeks to eliminate disparities in insurance coverage between mental health services and other medical treatments.

The MHPAEA has been a crucial step in improving millions of Americans' access to mental health and substance use disorder services. It helps reduce financial barriers and ensures that people receive the necessary care for their mental health needs, promoting overall well-being and better health outcomes.

The MHPAEA requires that insurance plans, both group and individual, that offer mental health and substance use disorder benefits must provide coverage comparable to their coverage for medical and surgical benefits. This means that:

- **FINANCIAL REQUIREMENTS:** The MHPAEA prohibits imposing higher copayments, coinsurance, deductibles, or out-of-pocket maximums for mental health and SUD services compared to medical services.

- **TREATMENT LIMITATIONS:** It prevents insurance plans from applying stricter limitations on the number of visits or days of coverage for mental health and SUD treatment than they do for medical treatments.

Every Student Succeeds Act (2015)

The Every Student Succeeds Act (ESSA) replaced the No Child Left Behind Act (NCLB) and introduced several significant changes to federal education policy. It represents a shift toward more state and local control in education policy, providing greater flexibility while saying all students have access to a high-quality education.

The key features are:

- **STATE AND LOCAL CONTROL:** Provides states with greater flexibility in designing their accountability systems, setting academic standards, and determining school improvement strategies.

- **ACCOUNTABILITY AND ASSESSMENT:** ESSA maintains the requirement for annual assessments in English language arts and math for students in grades 3-8 and once in high school. However, it gives states the flexibility to design their own accountability systems, including additional indicators of school quality or student success beyond test scores.

- **SCHOOL IMPROVEMENT:** States must develop comprehensive plans to improve struggling schools, including those with persistent achievement gaps.

- **SUPPORT FOR EARLY CHILDHOOD EDUCATION:** Allows states to use federal funds to expand access to preschool programs for low-income children.

- **TITLE I FUNDING:** Includes provisions to ensure that federal funds are targeted to the schools and students with the greatest need.

- **ENGLISH LEARNERS:** Provides support for professional development for teachers working with ELs and encourages meaningful engagement of families.

- **TEACHER QUALITY AND PROFESSIONAL DEVELOPMENT:** The law also emphasizes supporting effective instructional practices and using evidence-based strategies.

Landmark Cases

Landmark cases are critical in shaping the legal landscape of a country or jurisdiction. These cases significantly impact society and can bring about substantial changes in laws, policies, and the interpretation of the Constitution. Here are some essential reasons why landmark cases are crucial:

- **SETTING PRECEDENT:** Landmark cases often establish legal precedents that guide future court decisions. Once a court has ruled on a fundamental legal issue, lower courts are likely to follow the same reasoning in similar cases, providing consistency and predictability in the legal system.

- **CLARIFYING AMBIGUOUS LAWS:** Landmark cases help clarify laws that may be ambiguous or open to interpretation.

- **ADVANCING CIVIL RIGHTS:** Many landmark cases involve civil rights issues and have played a vital role in advancing equality and social justice.

- **PROTECTING INDIVIDUAL LIBERTIES:** Landmark cases can protect individual rights and liberties by defining the limits of government power and preventing potential abuses. Cases involving issues like freedom of speech, privacy, and due process have safeguarded individual freedoms.

- **PROMOTING SOCIAL CHANGE:** Some landmark cases have driven social change and progressive reforms. They can be catalysts for challenging outdated or discriminatory practices and encouraging societal progress.

- **INFLUENCING LEGISLATION:** Landmark cases may prompt legislators to enact new laws or amend existing ones to reflect the court's decisions or address issues highlighted by the case.

- **ENCOURAGING PUBLIC DISCOURSE:** Landmark cases often spark public discourse and raise awareness about significant legal, social, or moral issues.

- **STRENGTHENING THE RULE OF LAW:** Landmark cases contribute to the rule of law by ensuring that even the most powerful entities, including governments and corporations, are subject to the same legal principles as individuals.

Brown v. Board of Education (1954)

African American students were often forced to attend separate, inferior schools. The case arose when a group of African American parents, led by Oliver Brown, challenged the segregation policy in Topeka, Kansas.

The ruling overturned the previous "separate but equal" doctrine established in the 1896 case Plessy v. Ferguson, which had allowed for racial segregation as long as separate facilities were deemed equal. The Brown decision set a new legal precedent, marking a pivotal moment in the civil rights movement and paving the way for the desegregation of schools and other public institutions across the United States. It was a significant step toward promoting equality in education.

Regarding special education: This case was the basis for striking down local laws that excluded children with disabilities from schools and established that children with disabilities have the right to public education.

Tinker v. Des Moines Independent Community School District (1969)

Although not specific to special needs, this case established an important precedent for students' First Amendment rights in the school setting. It recognized that students have the right to express their opinions and engage in peaceful symbolic speech as long as it does not materially interfere with the educational environment or the rights of others. This case has had a lasting impact on the interpretation of free speech rights for students in public schools and the ability to advocate for students.

P.A.R.C. v. Commonwealth of Pennsylvania (1972)

Mills v. Board of Education (1972)

At the time, millions of children with disabilities were refused enrollment in public schools, received inadequate services by public schools, or sent to institutions. These cases addressed the denial of education to students with disabilities.

The court ruled that all children, regardless of their disabilities, have a right to free appropriate public education. This case contributed to developing and passing federal legislation, such as the Education for All Handicapped Children Act.

Hudson v. Rowley (1982)

The case involved the question of what constitutes an appropriate education for students with disabilities. The decision established that an appropriate education for students with disabilities does not necessarily mean providing the best or optimal education possible. Instead, it focuses on providing educational services and accommodations that enable students to progress and benefit from their education. This case set a precedent for determining the appropriateness of educational services by providing the "basic floor of opportunity" under IDEA and held that schools must merely provide "some educational benefit" for children with disabilities.

Honig v. Doe (1988)

The case addressed the issue of disciplining students with disabilities and their right to receive a free appropriate public education.

The case established an important precedent regarding the discipline of students with disabilities. It clarified that students with disabilities are protected under the IDEA and cannot be excluded from school based on their disability-related behaviors. The ruling reinforced the rights of students with disabilities to receive appropriate educational services. It highlighted the importance of addressing behavioral issues through positive interventions and supports rather than punitive measures.

Endrew F. v. Douglas County School District (2017)

The school district argued that as long as the IEP provided some educational benefit, it satisfied the FAPE standard. On the other hand, Endrew F.'s parents argued for a higher standard, asserting that an IEP should provide a meaningful educational benefit.

The Court held that under the IDEA, schools must provide a reasonably calculated education to enable a child to make progress in light of the child's circumstances. In other words, the IEP must offer a more substantive and meaningful educational program that is tailored to the unique needs of the student.

This case may be one of the most important special education cases in decades, as the Court decided that IDEA requires meaningful benefits. We just don't know what "meaningful" means.

THE SECRET AUTISM ROADMAP

IEPs

IEP

"I Expect Progress"

— Author Unknown

THE SECRET

The secret is school districts don't give away good programs. They don't evaluate the student, determine what they need, and provide it. Instead, the school typically has a series of programs that are not intensive enough to provide for anything more than minimal gains. The IEP instead requires you to convince the school district what is the right program for your child. You can only do that when your evaluation and goals point them in that direction.

My experience as a parent and advocate has shown me that public schools will try to get away with as much as possible. I've dealt with numerous cases when they prefer to give up on students and house them in special education with no real education benefit. So I suggest always mainstreaming your child with only a few pull-out services. School districts love to tell you they can work on all the social issues in a special education classroom. Then later, your child can go into a special education classroom, but the second your child is put full-time in a special education classroom, there is very little chance they will ever come out. In these situations, you need to request a 1on1 aide. Public school aides are usually horrible, so document, document, and push for an outside ABA vendor to be your child's 1-on-1 aide in the classroom.

Another vital element is to have open communication. Have it written into your IEP so you can communicate regularly with all teachers, therapists, and aides. You should create a communication folder that follows your child that all teachers, therapists, and aides can write in so you know what is happening daily and can quickly address and assist your child as needed.

The IEP Roadmap

School districts possess a high level of expertise in IEPs. They undergo extensive training from professionals and have a deep understanding of the IEP process, which allows them to optimize the benefits for the school district. They put considerable resources into developing what sounds like impressive programs. However, most of their programs don't come close to matching their description. As a parent, it is essential to familiarize yourself with the IEP process to effectively advocate for your child's needs and ensure their concerns are adequately addressed.

By understanding the IEP process, you become empowered to ask the right questions at the right time and can hold the school district accountable. By gaining insights into each component of the IEP process, you can grasp its significance and ensure that every aspect genuinely caters to your child's individual concerns. This proactive approach will make it challenging for the school district to defend all the inadequacies in their programs.

PART 01 | REQUESTING AN EVALUATION

PART 02 | THE IEP NOTICE

PART 03 | WHO IS INVOLVED IN AN IEP

PART 04 | PARENT'S RIGHTS

PART 05 | THE EVALUATION

PART 06 | PRESENT LEVELS OF ACADEMIC AND FUNCTIONAL PERFORMANCE

PART 07 | GOALS AND OBJECTIVES

PART 08 | SPECIAL EDUCATION & RELATED SERVICES

PART 09 | ACCOMMODATIONS AND MODIFICATIONS

PART 10 | PLACEMENT

PART 11 | REVIEWING AND SIGNING THE IEP

What is an IEP?

An IEP plan is an Individualized Education Program developed for students with special needs. It is a legally binding document that outlines the specific educational goals, accommodations, and services that a student with a disability requires to progress in their education.

Who Qualifies for an IEP Plan?

To qualify for an IEP, a student must have a disability that meets the criteria in the Individuals with Disabilities Education Act. IDEA defines a "child with a disability" as someone who:

- Has a physical or mental impairment that affects their ability to learn, and

- Requires special education and related services to make progress in school.

There are 13 categories of disabilities that are eligible for special education and related services under IDEA, which include:

- Autism
- Emotional disturbance
- Hearing impairment
- Multiple Disabilities
- Other Health Impairment (e.g., ADHD, asthma)
- Speech or Language Impairment
- Visual Impairment
- Deaf-blindness
- Deafness
- Intellectual Disability
- Orthopedic impairment
- Specific Learning Disability (e.g., dyslexia, dyscalculia)
- Traumatic brain injury

What is a Section 504 Plan?

Similar to an IEP, a Section 504 plan lists the accommodations an eligible student would receive. It is individualized and based on the specific needs of the student's disability. Eligible students only receive services through general education programs or general education-funded programs.

Who Qualifies for a Section 504 Plan?

A student must be determined to: (1) have a physical or mental impairment that substantially limits one or more major life activities [learning is considered a major life activity]; or (2) have a record of such an impairment; or (3) be regarded as having such an impairment."

An important consideration in determining eligibility is clarifying the specific problem students might have that would qualify them for a 504 plan. Examples of substantial life functions that, if impaired, would trigger an individual's eligibility include breathing, walking, talking, seeing, hearing, learning, and taking care of oneself. Here are the most common 504 Plan qualifications:

- ADHD/ADD
- AIDS
- Allergies
- Anxiety
- Arthritis
- Asthma
- Bipolar Disorder
- Cancer
- Cerebral Palsy
- Cystic Fibrosis
- Diabetes
- Drugs & Alcohol

- Dyslexia
- Emotional Disturbance
- Encopresis/ Enuresis
- Epilepsy
- Hearing Impairment
- Hemophilia
- Learning Disability
- Leukemia
- Nut Allergies
- Obesity

- Orthopedic Impairment
- Skin Disorder
- Special Healthcare Needs
- Tourette's Syndrome
- Trauma
- Traumatic Brain Injury (TBI)
- Tuberculosis
- Visual Impairment

Why is the IEP so Confusing?

The IEP is a confusing, legally binding document that outlines a lot of information and is designed by a large committee with different objectives. Many sections use vague or confusing terms. The structure and design of the IEP isn't conducive to understanding its goals, and the goals are often difficult to understand or measure.

On top of that the IEP is often revised and updated on an annual basis. New information is added in a haphazard way over old information. Questions and concerns by parents are never truly clarified or documented. Overall IEPs are difficult for people knowledgeable in IEPs to understand and almost impossible for parents and students to understand.

The following sections will break down the IEP process into the required legal steps it follows, with tips and suggestions on how to improve the IEP process to improve the outcome of the IEP.

TIPS for Before the IEP

Remember, each IEP meeting is an opportunity to advocate for your child's needs. Be proactive, ask questions, and participate in the process to ensure the best outcomes for your child.

- **REQUEST A DRAFT IEP:** Ask the school to provide a draft of the proposed IEP before the meeting so you have time to review and prepare your input.

- **REQUEST ADDITIONAL EVALUATIONS IF NECESSARY:** If you believe your child's needs have changed or if you have concerns not adequately addressed or don't feel the school evaluation was complete, request additional evaluations.

- **ORGANIZE RELEVANT DOCUMENTS:** Gather all documents related to your child's education, including progress reports, previous IEPs, and work samples. Keep them organized and easy to access.

- **WRITE DOWN YOUR CONCERNS, GOALS, AND QUESTIONS:** List your concerns, programs that haven't been working, questions regarding your child's progress, and include proposed goals you would like to achieve.

- **ADDRESS BEHAVIORAL CONCERNS:** If your child has behavioral challenges, discuss strategies and supports to address those concerns within the IEP.

- **BE AN ACTIVE PARTICIPANT:** Take an active role during the meeting by asking questions, seeking clarification, and providing input on proposed goals and services.

- **BRING A SUPPORT PERSON:** Consider having a trusted friend, family member, or advocate accompany you to the IEP meeting.

- **ADVOCATE FOR APPROPRIATE ACCOMMODATIONS AND MODIFICATIONS:** Ensure that appropriate accommodations and modifications are included in the IEP to support your child's access to the curriculum.

- **SEEK CLARITY ON SERVICES AND SUPPORTS:** Understand the type, frequency, and duration of services and supports your child will receive, such as specialized instruction, speech therapy, or occupational therapy.

- **REQUEST PROGRESS MONITORING AND COMMUNICATION PLAN:** Discuss how your child's progress will be monitored and how you will be regularly informed of their achievements and challenges.

- **REVIEW AND SIGN THE FINAL IEP:** Thoroughly review the finalized IEP, ensuring that it accurately reflects the decisions made during the meeting, and sign it once you are satisfied. If not, only approve what you want and deny what you don't.

IEP PART 1 | Requesting an Evaluation

Often times an IEP is started by requesting an evaluation for a learning disability. Maybe your child is struggling in school, and you suspect they have a learning disability. They may be getting sent to the office regularly. A parent or teacher can make a request to the school for an evaluation for special education services, but often these concerns are brushed off by the school district.

How to Request an Evaluation for Special Education

A common mistake is making a request for an evaluation in person. Maybe while talking to a principal or counselor. They might recommend waiting to see how the year goes or will, ask if there are problems at home or will suggest a tutor. These are common tactics that school districts will use to delay the process.

THE PROPER WAY TO REQUEST AN EVALUATION:

- Email the school administrator, special education director or principal. Explain your concerns and request an assessment for a learning disability.

- Once the school receives the email, they must send your proposed assessment plan within 15 days. This is often ignored so follow-up is required, or you will receive a phone call to talk you out of an assessment.

- The assessment plan must specify the types of assessments to be conducted. It must also state that no special education services will result from the assessment without your written consent.

TIPS: It is very easy to get frustrated when dealing with someone at your child's school, specifically when discussing problems regarding your child and trying to resolve them. When you write letters, try to stay calm. State the facts without letting anger, frustration, blame, or other negative emotions take over.

- When you write letters to a school as if they are going to a stranger.

- Please write your email and let it sit a day before sending it. You might have forgotten some important detail or just to clarify the letter.

- Have someone else read it over.

- Keep a record for yourself. Emails work great in that way.

Sample Letter/Email

Requesting an evaluation for special education services

Dear (school administrator, special education director or principal),

I am requesting that my child, (child's name), be evaluated for special education services. I am worried that (child's name) is not doing well in school and believe they may need special services to learn. (Child's name) is in the (_) grade at (name of school). (Teacher's name) is their teacher.

Note: If your child has been identified as having a disability by professionals outside the school system, add the following sentence to the end of the first paragraph: "(Child's name) has been identified as having (name of disability) by (name of professional). Enclosed is a copy of the report(s) I have received that explains (child's name) condition."

Specifically, I am worried because (child's name) does/does not (give a few direct examples of your child's problems at school).

We have tried the following to help (child's name): (If you or the school have done anything extra to help your child, briefly state it here).

Please let me know what type of assessments will be used before the evaluation begins. If you have any questions, please email me.

Thank you for your prompt attention to my request.

Sincerely,

Your name

cc: your child's principal (if the letter is addressed to an administrator) and your child's teacher(s)

The IEP invitation is a request for you to attend an IEP meeting. The IEP should include, date, time, place, purpose, and people invited.

Can't make the date?

If you can't attend the IEP on the date the school provided, write the school and tell them NOT to hold the meeting without you and offer them three dates and times you can attend and IEP. You can also ask to attend the IEP by video or on the phone.

Don't speak English?

You can request an interpreter.

NOTICE OF SPECIAL EDUCATION IEP/PLACEMENT MEETING

Date_____

To:_____
Parent and Student (if postsecondary goals and transition services are being considered)

An Individualized Education Program (IEP) Team meeting for your child has been scheduled for
_____at_____at _____
Date   Time   Location
You are invited and strongly encouraged to participate in this meeting. If you are unable to attend on this date or location, you are encouraged to request to reschedule the meeting. You may also request another method of participation (e.g. conference call).

The purpose(s) of this meeting is to:
- [ ] Determine or re-determine eligibility
- [ ] Consider special education placement
- [ ] Develop an Individualized Education Program (IEP), if appropriate
- [ ] Review/amend the IEP and/or placement (annual review or other review)
- [ ] Consider postsecondary goals and transition services (prior to entry to high school or age 16)
- [ ] Consider the need for reevaluation
- [ ] Review the results of recent evaluation(s)
- [ ] Consider the need for a functional behavior assessment and/or develop/revise a behavior intervention plan
- [ ] Other_____

The following people have been invited to attend the meeting:

Required members: If any required members are unable to attend, the parent will be notified and asked to provide written consent for excusal.		Additional members who may attend: These members do not require an excusal.	
Title	Name (optional)	Title	Name (optional)
☐ LEA Representative			
☐ Special Ed. Teacher			
☐ General Ed. Teacher			
☐ Student (if transition to be discussed)			

If transition is being discussed and another agency is likely to be providing or paying for services, a representative from that agency will be invited with the consent of parent or student, if age 18 or older. For children previously served in Babies Can't Wait, you may request a representative of that agency attend to assist with transition services. You may also invite other individuals who have knowledge or special expertise regarding your child. If you are unable to attend the IEP meeting, a copy of the IEP will be mailed to you.

Sincerely,

_____   _____
Name   *Phone/Email*

PLEASE COMPLETE AND RETURN THIS SECTION TO YOUR CHILD'S TEACHER OR SCHOOL BY_____.

Child's Name:_____

- [ ] I will attend the meeting as scheduled on_____
- [ ] I would like to reschedule the meeting or arrange for an alternate means of participation. Please contact me at_____
- [ ] I am unable to attend the meeting. The meeting may proceed without me. I understand that I will receive a copy of the IEP and any other documents. I can have these documents explained to me if I request the system to explain them.
- [ ] I consent to the invitation of the agency representative listed above that is likely to be responsible for providing or paying for transition services.

_____   _____   _____
Parent   Phone/Email   Date

There are Four Reasons for an IEP:

PARENT REQUEST/SCHOOL DISTRICT REQUEST: A parent can request an Individualized Education Plan (IEP) for their child whenever they feel there are problems with the IEP.

ANNUAL GOALS REVIEW: The IEP team meets at least once a year to review the student's progress toward their goals and objectives and to make any necessary changes to the IEP.

TRI-ANNUAL EVALUATION: The team comprehensively re-evaluates the student's needs at least once every three years or more often if necessary.

TRANSITION SERVICES: For students aged 16 or older, the team develops a plan for the student's transition from school to post-secondary life, including post-secondary education, employment, and independent living.

Information to Include with the IEP invitation.

When returning the IEP, it is always a good idea to include a few requests. In many situations, requests can be written right on the IEP notice and returned to the

Request All reports or Evaluations 3-5 days before the IEP

Example: Please provide all reports, evaluations, draft goals, or anything else being presented at the IEP at least 3 to 5 days before the IEP.

Inform the school at least 24 hours prior to the IEP that you will be recording the IEP.

Example: I will be audio recording the IEP meeting on (date of IEP). Please ensure that all participants receive prior notice of this intent to record.

Inform the school if you will be bringing someone to an IEP meeting.

No requirement in IDEA states that a parent needs to inform the district if they bring a friend, coach, or advocate. If you can, it is helpful to let the district know whom you're bringing, but you do not have to.

Should you record the IEP Meeting?

The correct answer should always be yes. A recording of an IEP meeting can be helpful as your memory aid. It is also powerful evidence that helps you hold the district accountable. The district won't be able to deny something a representative said, nor can they fail to put a service or accommodation into place that was agreed upon in the meeting.

Numerous times I've read IEP notes and realized they were highly slanted. Parental concerns were barely mentioned. Programs described in detail during the IEP had no real resemblance to the actual program.

Federal law allows a parent to record IEP meetings as long as they give 24 hours' notice. But a school can have a policy that prohibits parents from recording meetings. If so, that policy must include exceptions to ensure parents understand the IEP.

PARENT(S)	One or both of the child's parents or caregiver.
PARENT'S FRIEND, ADVOCATE, OR SPECIALIST	Parents can invite a friend, advocate, or specialist.
STUDENT (As Appropriate)	When appropriate, which is very rarely or never. If the school brings your child to an IEP, it is best to say hi and let the team know is can go back to class
SCHOOL DISTRICT REPRESENTATIVE	A person from the school district who can authorize funds to provide the services for a student's needs.
SCHOOL DISTRICT REPRESENTATIVE THAT CAN INTERPRET ASSESSMENTS	This person has the knowledge to interpret the school's assessments.
SPECIAL ED TEACHER	At least one special education teacher or service provider.
GENERAL ED TEACHER	At least one general education teacher.
TRANSITION SERVICE REPRESENTATIVE	Responsible for planning, implementing, and evaluating transition services at the school level.

Parents Play an Important Role in the IEP

If you're new to special education, you may wonder what your role is as a parent or caregiver. At times it will feel like you are powerless in the process. You may not be an expert in special education or understand the available resource, but you play a crucial role.

You're an equal member of the IEP team.

The Individuals with Disabilities Act puts the parents at the top of the list of required IEP team members. That isn't a mistake. As a member of the IEP team, you play an essential part in deciding how your child will be taught. This included which classroom and which services your child needs. The school also can't change the IEP without allowing you to challenge those changes.

You know and understand your child.

The school only knows your child as a student. One of many often only knows them on paper, such as test results or other documents. You can provide a bigger picture. You might see things in your child that the school misses. There are many kids with very noticeable concerns, but many more are silent. They will sit in the class and will never cause disruption but are having obvious academic difficulties.

You keep an eye on your child's services and supports.

The IEP team is supposed to tailor support and services to meet your child's specific needs. But busy special education departments may try to use a "standard" set of supports and assistance for all students with a particular disability. Or services are regularly canceled for no real reason. As a parent or caregiver, you can ensure the IEP is designed with your child in mind, implemented, and followed through on.

You are not an employee of the school.

In most cases, you are not an employee of the school district. Employees are very hesitant to admit their programs are appropriate. There have been numerous cases of special education teachers being terminated for advocating for special needs children, making it extremely important for parents to advocate for their child vigorously.

School District IEP Tactics

School districts are experts at IEPs. They conduct numerous IEPs a year and attend seminars and training sessions on how to conduct IEPs to benefit the school district. Saying that often most people with minimal IEP experience will attend the IEP and follow the school district's lead. Here are some of the school district's most common tactics:

School District will only say positive comments.

This is a form of gaslighting to make you question your child's behavior. This is easily overcome by listing your concerns, emails or concerns from staff, and work samples.

"His grades are fine!"

"We like him!"

"He's doing well academically."

"We've never seen him do that at school."

"I can't make that decision, I have to ask...."

The School District Avoids Answering Questions.

A common problem is school districts will talk but won't answer parents' concerns. They might throw around a lot of confusing jargon. They will also avoid writing down parental concerns or verbal commitments in an IEP. In many cases, they will just say to call an IEP if there is a problem.

TIPS:

· It is always a good idea to ask the school district to describe the program in detail and then ask to observe it.

· Another suggestion is to write out your concerns and ask for an answer.

· If they are using a lot of confusing jargon, stop them and ask them to explain it in clear language.

IEP doesn't have all the required people and doesn't follow the IEP process

IEP doesn't have all the required people and doesn't follow the IEP processThis often happens when schools try to keep IEP meetings very informal and avoid writing anything of significance into the IEP. It may be your first or second IEP. Everyone is very friendly and polite. Essential terms are downplayed. Everyone talks about helping the child, but nothing changes. The IEP requires specific people. There is an Excuse Rules for an IEP meeting, but the parents must agree to the exclusion of key people in writing.

IEP Intimidation

The school district will try to intimidate or bully the parent(s) by filling an IEP meeting with people and will talk over the parent during the IEP.

TIP: In this situation ask, "How does everyone at the meeting know or work with my child. If they don't have any knowledge, then request they be barred from the meeting.

The School District will say they don't have the money for that service or support.

Quite often parents will attend and IEP meeting but the student's needed services are denied. Sometimes parents are given the excuse of "no funding," or "we just don't have the resources." The parents trust the IEP team, but services and placement are legally decided by what the student needs, not on how much they cost. One of the benefits of recording IEPs is this can be quickly resolved.

Parent's Rights

Parent's Rights is an overview of your educational rights or procedural safeguards. They can be very helpful if there is a dispute. Here is a summary:

IDEA

Federal law requires school districts to provide a "free appropriate public education" (FAPE).

Parent Participation

Parents have the right to participate in any decision-making meeting regarding child's special education program.

Where To Go For Assistance

Contact your child's teacher, administrator staff in your school district, or your local plan area (SELPA).

Prior Written Notice

When the school district proposes a program change, they must notify you in writing prior to the change.

Parental Consent

You have the right to refer your child for special education services.

Required Approval

You must give written consent before your school district can provide services.

Parent Does Not Provide Consent?

If the parent does not consent, the school district may pursue the initial assessment by utilizing due process procedures.

Revoke Consent

Parents can revoke special education and services. It must be in writing.

Surrogate Parent Appointment

There must be an individual assigned to act as a surrogate parent for the parents of a child with a disability.

Nondiscriminatory Assessment

You have the right to have your child assessed in all areas of suspected disability that is not racially or sexually discriminatory.

Independent Educational Assessments

If you disagree with the results of an assessment, you have the right to ask for and obtain an IEE at public expense.

Access to Educational Records

You have a right to inspect and review your child's education records without delay.

HOW DISPUTES ARE RESOLVED

Due Process Hearing

You have the right to request an impartial due process hearing regarding the identification, assessment, and educational placement of your child or the provision of FAPE.

Alternative Dispute Resolution

You may request mediation either before or after a request for a due process hearing is made.

Pre-hearing Mediation Conference

You may seek a resolution through mediation prior to filing a request for a due process hearing.

Due Process Rights

A listing of your rights during a Due Process hearing.

Filing a Due Process Complaint

You need to file a written request for a due process hearing.

Resolution Session

Resolution sessions shall be convened within 15 days of receiving notice of the parent's due process hearing request.

Appealing Decision

The hearing decision is final and binding on both parties. Either party may appeal the hearing decision by filing a civil action in state or federal court within 90 days of the final decision.

SCHOOL DISCIPLINE

Suspension or Expelled

School personnel will consider on a case-by-case basis if a student violates the code of conduct rules. Change of setting can only happen for up to ten consecutive school days.

What Happens After Ten Days

If a child exceeds 10 days in such a placement, an IEP team meeting must be held to determine whether the disability causes the child's misconduct.

Misconduct Not Caused By Disability

If a child misconduct from the disability, disciplinary action, such as expulsion can take place.

ATTENDING PRIVATE SCHOOL

Parentally Placed in Private Schools

When parent(s) place their child in private schools, they might not have the right to special education and related services necessary to provide FAPE.

Private School Reimbursement

You must follow a process if you would like to be reimbursed for sending your child to a private school

State Compliance Complaint

You may file a state compliance complaint when you believe that a school district has violated federal or state special education laws or regulations.

State Compliance Complaints are a great way to resolve disputes.

They are much quicker and cheaper than a Due Process Hearing and they stay on the school's public record making.

IEP Tips

Ideally the questions you ask lead to a conclusion that will ensure your child's success. Below are general guidelines for ensuring a successful meeting:

You have finished the formalities of the IEP. Now the essential parts start.

- **STAY CALM.** Although you may be angry and frustrated, remain calm and in control at the meeting. Doing otherwise will likely provoke a defensive reaction that may not be in your child's best interest.

- **ASK QUESTIONS.** Ask how they came up with a certain conclusion. Ask if they collected data to be sure goals were met. Ask

- **ASK FOR SUGGESTIONS.** To generate new ideas or approaches from other team members, ask questions, keep people involved, and try to get them on your side. Teachers are on the front lines and will often tell you their concerns, so it is important to keep them involved.

- **ASK THEM TO CLARIFY.** IEPs are a world of their own with a lot of abbreviations, jargon, program names, and test you will be unfamiliar with. Always ask for clarification, paraphrase, and restate questions. Try to understand the philosophy behind the staff recommendations.

- **LIST AND STATE YOUR CONCERNS.** If something hasn't been working or you disagree, do not be afraid to ask again to negotiate an agreement. Prepare your questions and items to address.

- **TRY AND KEEP THE CONVERSATION CORDIAL.** Is someone yelling, bulldozing the conversation, or being disrespectful? Ask sk the facilitator to address the behavior through the school's "code of civility" or by rescheduling the IEP at a time when the person can maintain their composure. Make sure the behavior is well documented.

- **BRING COOKIES.** Bring a tray of cookies. If things get heated, offer cookies to the person.

- **BRING A PHOTO OF YOUR CHILD.** With a room full of adults, it is easy to forget what the objective of the meeting is.

- **TAKE A BREAK.** Sometimes everyone needs a few minutes to get some air or relax for a few minutes.

Giving Parental Input on the IEP

During the IEP, the facilitator gets to the Parent Input space in the IEP, they will turn to the parents and say, "Parents, what are your priorities and concerns for your child?" Most of the time, parents will be at a loss for words as many thoughts flood their mind. They'll start listing a few things off the top of their head. But in the end, the most important concerns will be left out because they weren't prepared to answer this question.

A parent input statement lets you share your most pressing concerns with your child's IEP team. It's a great way to document your child's strengths and struggles at school and at home. It is your chance to tell the team who your child is beyond their test scores and performance in school. Most importantly, clearly state your concerns. To ensure your insight are incorporated, write up your input and ask for it to be entered into the parental input space on the IEP.

Tips for Writing a Parental Input Statement

- **KEEP IT SHORT.** This letter isn't a legal document, so there is no special format you need to follow but aim for 1-page with bullet points and short statements, which is much easier to understand than lengthy paragraphs.

- **BE POLITE AND PROFESSIONAL.** You should raise issues respectfully and clearly.

- **USE FACTS AS MUCH AS POSSIBLE.** Try to avoid using emotionally charged statements. For example, instead of, "I am furious because he comes home upset every day," try writing, "Every day Daniel comes home upset and in tears. When I ask him why he says that XYZ is happening during the school day. We need to add a solution to his IEP to prevent this."

- **DISCUSS WHAT STRATEGIES ARE WORKING.** This is where you can highlight what academic or behavioral methods are working.

- **CLEARLY STATE YOUR CONCERNS.** Be sure to mention any and all educational, functional, social, behavioral, and health concerns you have.

- **GIVE RECOMMENDATIONS.** Simply pointing out all of the flaws is important, but what's even more important is naming possible solutions.

When you feel problems with the IEP's implementation or effectiveness, it is extremely important to start documenting all your concerns. This documented statement can serve as proof of any objections or concerns you have should any issues come up in due process.

The evaluation is very important. It determines the goals, supports, and services the child will need to access a Free and Appropriate Education (FAPE). It is best to begin developing an appropriate IEP by starting with a good evaluation. When an IEP is developed that is based on a faulty or incomplete evaluation, you will need a lot of help to overcome that and create reasonable goals, supports, and services.

▶ Evaluation

Determinations
Eligibility

Explain Present
Levels

▶ Goals

Goals are Based
on the Evaluation

▶ Services

Goals Determine what
Services are Needed

Goals Determine
Accommodations and
Placements

The IEP members, including the parents or guardians, will review the evaluation results and determines if the student is eligible for special education services and what goals, services, and supports will be included.

An Independent Educational Evaluation (IEE)

When the school district conducts student evaluations, the district employs evaluators. Quite often, their process for an evaluation can take months, and they often use methods that don't get an accurate evaluation of the child. From insufficient tests, poor data, or come to inappropriate conclusions. These evaluations will stay in your child's academic record.

On the other hand, IEEs often give a much more comprehensive report of a student's abilities and challenges. Parental concerns are often given much more credibility.

In many cases, the Independent Evaluator can attend the IEP to explain their results and provide program recommendations.

Requesting an IEE

If a parent disagrees with an evaluation from a school district they have the right to an independent educational evaluation at public expense

Steps for Requesting an IEE

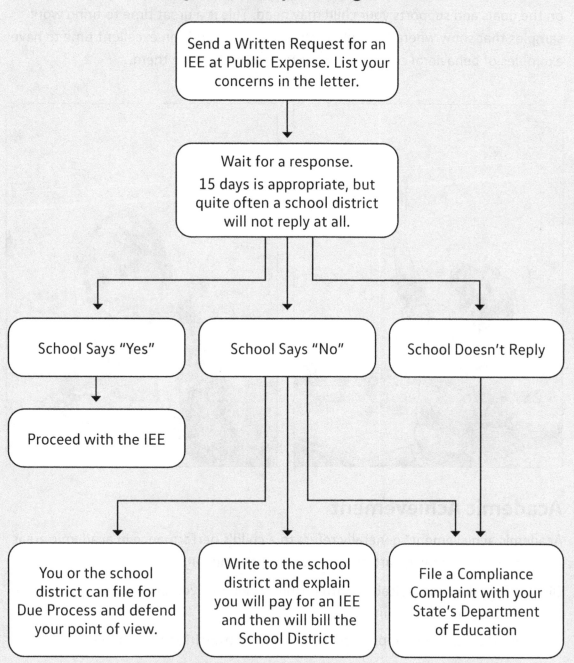

Send a Written Request for an IEE at Public Expense. List your concerns in the letter.

Wait for a response.
15 days is appropriate, but quite often a school district will not reply at all.

School Says "Yes"

School Says "No"

School Doesn't Reply

Proceed with the IEE

You or the school district can file for Due Process and defend your point of view.

Write to the school district and explain you will pay for an IEE and then will bill the School District

File a Compliance Complaint with your State's Department of Education

Be persistent. School districts have commonly been known to drag the requests for an Independent Evaluation out for years.

Using the evaluation, the team identifies the student's strengths, weaknesses, and current academic and functional levels. This part of the IEP is used to start deciding on the goals and supports your child may need. This is a great time to bring work samples that show where the child is struggling. Also, it is an excellent time to have examples of behavioral concerns and how to accommodate them.

Academic Achievement

Academic achievement" generally refers to a child's performance in academic areas (e.g., reading or language arts, math, science, and history.)

Discuss how the child's disability affects his or her involvement and progress in the general education curriculum:

- works better when prompts are given for transition from subjects
- requires a quiet area for testing
- needs assistance with visual schedules and graphic organizers
- requires visual or written instructions rather than auditory

Functional Performance

This term is generally understood as referring to "skills or activities that are not considered academic but also need to be addressed in the school setting.

- requires earplugs or noise-canceling headsets in hallways or lunchroom
- social skills, such as making friends and communicating with others
- behavior skills, such as knowing how to behave across a range of settings
- mobility skills, such as walking, getting around, going up and down stairs
- assistance during special activities or assemblies
- a quiet area where the student can take a time-out if necessary

Goals and Objectives are one of the most critical portions of the IEP. There is a term that **"GOALS DEFINE SERVICES."** That means if you have only 2 or 3 goals, you will only receive services to achieve those 2 or 3 goals. This is the time to make sure you have all the goals needed to accomplish all of your objectives with targeted support tailored to your child's specific needs.

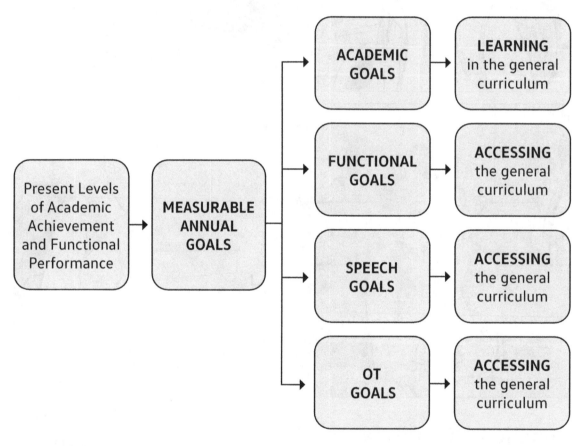

IEPs MUST MEET MORE THAN MINIMAL GAINS

The 2017 U.S. Supreme Court ruling, Endrew F. v. Douglas County School District, states IEP goals need to provide much more than minimal gain:

If that is not a reasonable prospect for a child, his IEP need not aim for grade-level advancement. But his educational program must be ambitious in light of his circumstances, just as advancement from grade to grade is appropriate for most children in the regular classroom. The goals may differ, but every child should have the chance to meet challenging objectives.

The first step in developing IEP Goals is to evaluate ALL the child's areas of need. Here is a break down of the most common areas of need:

ACADEMIC GOALS

READING FLUENCY

READING COMPREHENSION

WRITTEN EXPRESSION

ORGANIZATION SKILLS

FUNCTIONAL MATH

FUNCTIONAL GOALS

SOCIAL SKILLS

SELF REGULATION

ORGANIZATIONAL SKILLS

RESTRICTED INTERESTS

EXECUTIVE FUNCTIONING

SPEECH GOALS

ARTICULATION

FLUENCY

RECEPTIVE LANGUAGE

EXPRESSIVE LANGUAGE

PRAGMATICS

OT GOALS

FINE MOTOR SKILLS

GROSS MOTOR SKILLS

SENSORY PROCESSING

VISUAL MOTOR INTEGRATION

The next few pages will break these down into more specifics.

ACADEMIC GOALS GRADE LEVEL IEP GOALS

Academic goals are specific educational targets designed to meet the unique goals in any academic area depending on the student's needs and areas of difficulty. Here are a few academic areas that should be covered:

READING FLUENCY:

- Decoding
- Inferences
- Vocabulary

READING COMPREHENSION:

- Explaining What They Read
- Create Visual of What They Read
- Predict What Will Happen
- Summarize A Story
- Make a Connection with the Story
- Identifying Main Ideas, Characters and Story Lines
- Active Reading

WRITTEN EXPRESSION:

- Develop Ideas for an Essay
- Create an outline
- Write an Essay with Correct Spelling, Punctuation, and Grammar
- Generate Diagrams, Learning Logs, Journals, and Note-taking
- Revise Writing

ORGANIZATION:

- Explaining What They Read
- Create Visual, Charts, and Schedules for Organization
- Note-taking

FUNCTIONAL MATH:

- Understanding Measurements
- Number Sense
- Ability to count verbally (first forward, then backward)
- Spatial awareness, visualizing what "3" of something looks like.
- More than, less than
- Matching sets
- patterns
- estimating
- sequences
- problem-solving
- comparison
- sorting
- language
- working memory
- Money Skills IEP Goals
- Reading Comprehension on Math Word Problems

FUNCTIONAL GOALS

Functional goals address a wide range of areas, including social skills, communication, behavior, mobility, self-care, and vocational skills, depending on the student's individual needs. Here are a few areas that should be covered:

SOCIAL SKILLS:

- Understanding their emotions and other's emotions
- Understanding others body language and monitoring their own
- Understanding facial expressions during conversations
- Initiating (in social situations)
- Maintaining (friendships and conversations)
- Responding (to another person's initiation)
- Understanding and using nonverbal communication
- Pragmatic Language — Beginning and Ending Conversations, Topic Maintenance
- Awareness during social situations
- Perspective taking
- Problem-solving

SELF REGULATION:

- Utilizing relaxation techniques and other strategies for staying calm
- Recognizing frustration and take breaks when frustrated or upset

ORGANIZATIONAL SKILLS:

- Attention to Task
- Finishing Tasks
- Working Independently
- Managing Materials
- Transitioning Between Tasks
- Problem Solving
- Error Correcting (correcting own mistakes)
- Asking for Help When Necessary

RESTRICTED INTERESTS:

- Increase flexibility
- Tolerate changes in schedules and activities
- Increase the length of time for non-preferred subjects/activities
- Accepting mistakes of self and others

EXECUTIVE FUNCTIONING:

- Task analysis and planning
- Cognitive-behavioral strategies
- Sensory strategies
- Mindfulness practices
- Memory and attention exercises

SPEECH GOALS

Speech goals are specific objectives developed by a speech-language pathologist (SLP) to help students with a communication disorder improve their speech and language skills.

IMPROVE ARTICULATION

- Articulation refers to the ability to produce sounds correctly and use them to form words and sentences.

INCREASE FLUENCY

- Fluency refers to the ability to speak smoothly and without hesitation.

ENHANCE VOICE QUANTITIES

- Voice refers to the way that sound is produced and resonates.

DEVELOP RECEPTIVE LANGUAGE

- The ability to understand and comprehend language.

BUILD EXPRESSIVE LANGUAGE

- The ability to use words and sentences to express thoughts and ideas.

PRAGMATICS

- Pragmatics refers to the ability to use language in social situations.

OCCUPATIONAL THERAPY GOALS

OT goals are specific objectives developed by an occupational therapist to help a student with a disability develop the skills needed to perform daily activities, such as dressing, eating, and writing.

FINE MOTOR SKILLS:

- Working on tasks like writing, using scissors, buttoning clothes, and manipulating small objects.

GROSS MOTOR SKILLS:

- Working on tasks such as running, jumping, climbing stairs, and sports.

SENSORY PROCESSING:

- Working on ways to help process and responds to sensory information.

VISUAL MOTOR INTEGRATION:

- Working on improving the body's ability to coordinate the visual and motor systems.

How to Write an IEP Goals

An Individualized Education Program goal is a specific objective developed for a student with disabilities as part of their individualized education plan. IEP goals are designed to address the student's unique needs and outline what the student is expected to achieve within a specific timeframe, typically for a school year.

The goals are typically written using the SMART framework. This ensures that the goals are clear, measurable, realistic, relevant to the student'seducation, and have a specific time line for achievement.

What is achievable?

Every child is different, but goals should be significant. As the 2017 Supreme Court ruling decided, goals should be appropriately ambitious. It is much better to have an ambitious goal and come close than an easily achievable goal.

S	**SPECIFIC** Write a specific goal statement
M	**MEASURABLE** Identify measurable objectives
A	**ACHIEVABLE** Determine the criteria for success
R	**RELEVANT** Ensure relevance to the student's needs
T	**TIMELY** Include a timeline

PART 1 **STUDENT WILL**	PART 2 **SPECIFICS**	PART 4 **SUPPORTS**
(GOAL) Name the specific skill (academic or social) the child will master.	**(GOAL SPECIFICS)** Include the specifics of what is included in the goal.	**(ACCOMMODATIONS)** What sort of prompts, supports, or accommodations will be included.
PART 4 **ASSESSMENTS**	PART 5 **WHEN**	PART 6 **MEASUREMENT**
(HOW WILL IT BE MEASURED) Include how the goal will be measured, and who will be doing the assessments.	**(TIME FRAME)** When will data be collected or assessments completed. (daily, weekly, monthly)	**(ACCURACY LEVELS)** Examples: 90% | 4 of 5 times on 3 attempts 80% | 3 of 5 times on 3 attempts 70% | 3 of 5 times on 5 attempts

Goals that aren't fully achieved can be rewritten and continued.

IEP Goal Bank Examples

Finding great pre-written goals has always been challenging with online goal banks. As you prepare for an IEP with goal suggestions, these goals are great starting points. These goals can be customized to meet the specific need of your child.

- **STATE DEPARTMENT OF EDUCATION:** Many state departments of education provides resources and templates for IEP goals.

- **SPECIAL EDUCATION WEBSITES:** Several websites provide pre-written IEP goals. Examples include Wrightslaw, Understood, A Day In Our Shoes, and the Council for Exceptional Children. For more information do a search for IEP goal bank.

IEP GOAL — ENGLISH | WRITTEN EXPRESSION
The Student will increase writing skills to (grade/proficiency level) in the area(s) of (Ideas and Content, Organization, Voice, Word Choice, Sentence Fluency, and Conventions) as measured by (State Scoring Guide, analysis of writing samples, diagnostic survey, and spelling inventory) by June (year).

IEP GOAL — MATH | MULTIPLICATION AND DIVISION
Use mental arithmetic, paper-and-pencil algorithms, and calculators to solve problems involving the multiplication of multidigit whole numbers by 2-digit whole numbers and the division of multidigit whole numbers by 1-digit whole numbers; describe the strategies used and explain how they work as measured by (State Scoring Guide) by June (year).

IEP GOAL — SOCIAL SKILLS
During recess, the student will initiate and begin a back and forth conversation exchange (for example, greeting and asking about a shared interest, such as a TV show, or asking if the peer enjoys crafts/art) with one of the previously identified classmates independently with 80% success across 3 consecutive weeks.

Organizing Goals

It is crucial to organize Goals and Objectives before the IEP. The Goals and Objectives section is often read off quickly and haphazardly, with goals being changed, removed, or updated quickly. It is essential to see the whole picture and ensure all the needed objectives are in place.

Try using a goal organization sheet to keep this part organized, figuring out how many goals were met and making sure new goals are added or partially met goals are updated.

GOALS AND OBJECTIVES

☐ New Goal

☐ Previous Goal

☐ Academic Goal

☐ Functional Behavior Goal

Annual Goal:

Time Frame:

Setting:

Assessment Type:

Accuracy Level:

Measured By:

☐ New Goal

☐ Previous Goal

☐ Academic Goal

☐ Functional Behavior Goal

Annual Goal:

Time Frame:

Setting:

Assessment Type:

Accuracy Level:

Measured By:

☐ New Goal

☐ Previous Goal

☐ Academic Goal

☐ Functional Behavior Goal

Annual Goal:

Time Frame:

Setting:

Assessment Type:

Accuracy Level:

Measured By:

☐ New Goal

☐ Previous G

Annual Goal:

IEP
PART
8

Special Education & Related Services

Once the IEP team has developed the annual goals for your child, the IEP team will begin talking about services, accommodations, modifications, and placement will be in place to make sure those goals can be reached. Special education directors describe this as a car. They will explain they don't have to provide a Cadillac of services, but they do have to provide services that work and are reliable and will achieve more than minimum gains.

What is the Least Restrictive Environment?

The least restrictive environment (LRE) means kids with special education should be in the same classrooms as other kids as much as possible. This is the best model for receiving an education. When children are only put in a general education classroom for an hour or two a day, they are not considered an actual member of the class and have additional difficulties socializing.

WHAT ARE PUSH-IN SERVICES?

Push-in services happen in the general education classroom. The general education teacher, special education teacher, and others (like speech therapists or occupational therapists) work collaboratively. This is called inclusive education.

WHAT ARE PULL-OUT SERVICES?

Pull-out services typically happen outside the general education classroom when the student goes to work one-on-one or in a small group setting.

WHAT ARE RELATED SERVICES?

Related services are additional services provided to students with disabilities to help them benefit from their special education program. They support the student's ability to access the curriculum and make progress toward their goals.

- Speech and language therapy
- Counseling or social work services
- Mobility services for students who are visually impaired

- Occupational therapy
- Assistive technology
- Transportation to and from school

Accommodations

- Extended time on tests and assignments
- Access to assistive technology,
- Preferential seating
- Breaks during class or testing
- Using visual aids or cue cards to reinforce important concepts
- Simplifying or rephrasing instructions or directions
- Providing written copies of oral presentations or lectures
- Providing a note-taker or recording lectures for later review.
- Sensory breaks
- Use of fidget toy
- Testing in a quiet area
- Extended test-taking time
- monthly, weekly, or bi-weekly parent conferences
- homework assignments chunked down to smaller tasks
- Adjusting the pacing of instruction
- Have the test read to them
- Able to answer verbally
- Extended time of tests or assignments

Modifications

Modifying the format of assignments, such as providing fill-in-the-blank worksheets or graphic organizers

- Changes in the level of difficulty or amount of work required
- Simplifying reading materials
- Allowing oral responses to written assignments or tests
- Modifying tests
- Adjusting grading criteria
- Allowing for alternative ways to demonstrate knowledge
- One-on-one or small-group instruction

WARNING:

Some modifications may affect the type of diploma a student is eligible to receive. For example, if a student uses modified assignments, they may not meet the requirements for a standard diploma. In these cases, the IEP team should work together to determine the best course of action and make decisions that support the student's long-term success.

Accommodations can Extend to College and College Testing

Colleges, universities, and college testing programs such as the SAT, or the ACT accept school accommodations. You will need to request the accommodations to make sure they are provided.

The participation of students with disabilities in general education is an important aspect of their educational experience and is the best way to keep students at grade level. The Individuals with Disabilities Education Act (IDEA) requires that students with disabilities be educated in the least restrictive environment possible, meaning they should be included in general education classes to the greatest extent appropriate.

Inclusion in the General Education Setting

Inclusion is not a legal term; it is a philosophy that refers to placing children with disabilities in their home schools, in the general education setting with supports, services, accommodations, and modifications that allow them to access the curriculum. The goal of including students with disabilities in general education is to promote their academic and social development, so it is imperative to provide appropriate supports. The most common problem is school districts don't want to provide appropriate supports and instead assign most of the the responsibilities to the general education teacher, who is leading lectures and working with numerous other children.

Extended School Year (ESY)

The extended school year is summer school. It helps the child retain their academic progress and speech and OT programs during the summer months.

What qualifies a student for ESY?

Federal regulations define extended school year services as "special education and related services that are provided to a child with a disability beyond the normal school year of the public agency and in accordance with the child's IEP." These services must be provided at no cost to the parent and meet state standards.

When determining eligibility for ESY services, the two most common things IEP teams will look at are:

- Whether or not the child is at risk of regressing or losing skills and knowledge during a break from school.

- Recoupment, meaning how long it might take for the child to regain the skills and knowledge they may have lost over the break.

IEP Transition Plan

An IEP transition plan is part of an Individualized Education Program that outlines the steps and services needed for a student with a disability to successfully transition from high school to post-secondary life. This plan is typically developed for students in their junior or senior year of high school and is designed to help them plan for their future after graduation.

The IEP transition plan is customized to the individual student and may include a variety of goals, such as:

- **ACADEMIC GOALS:** May identify the specific academic courses.

- **CAREER GOALS:** May outline the student's vocational or career goal.

- **INDEPENDENT LIVING GOALS:** May include goals related to living independently.

- **SOCIAL AND EMOTIONAL GOALS:** May address social and emotional needs.

Questions that Need to be Asked.

As the IEP team develops goals, supports, services, accommodations, and modifications, it is very important to ask lots of questions and let the school district answer them in detail. School districts have become very good at describing what seems like outstanding programs. Unfortunately, these programs rarely match their descriptions. Here are some open-ended questions to ask during the IEP to ensure you clearly understand the programs.

- When jargon or unfamiliar phrases are used, make sure to have it defined or explained to make sure everything is clear.

- Make sure goals aren't all being put on a teacher. Their primary the goal is to teach a classroom of kids, and can't be expected to handle the individual goals of a student.

- Have the school district describe any program they recommend in detail.

  - Have them walk through the program focusing on the strategies and processes the program uses and how and why they feel this would be an appropriate program for their child.
  - After the school has described the program, make sure to request the ability to observe the program.

Who will be delivering the services and supports? How often? When? Where? And with whom, if not a one-on-one or group aide?

I want to observe the proposed program and the teacher the school recommends.

Will we receive training or support to duplicate this program at home?

Could we walk through the current program and IEP plan piece by piece?

What sort of ongoing daily or weekly communication system will be used so we know what is going on at school?

Who are my contacts and resources available to access if I have questions or concerns about my child's education?

How will my child be included and supported during recesses, breaks, and activities?

What training will teachers and staff provide to ensure they can support my child's needs?

How often will I be receiving updates on how the program is working?

How quickly can the program be changed or updated if there are problems?

How and how often will the program be evaluated to determine progress?

Can we make a plan for keeping in touch in person about how everything is going?

You can express concerns before the programs begin by asking lots of questions. If or when the program appears unproductive, it allows you to push for outside agencies that are regularly more effective than school district programs.

After an IEP meeting, the district may ask you to sign the IEP — but you don't have to sign it immediately. A final review of the IEP is one of the most important parts of the IEP. Don't be rushed. Explain that once you receive the final IEP draft, you will need a week to review it.

You can sign the attendance list. You can include "participation only" after your name to ensure you haven't agreed to the IEP.

Steps to Finalizing the IEP

1 THE BENEFITS OF WAITING.

Schools often pressure you to sign the IEP as soon as possible, but waiting to sign the IEP also allows you to think over the IEP or have a friend or advocate read over the IEP. This waiting time can be very beneficial in developing a good IEP.

2 READ THE IEP

This might sound simple, but it is always recommended to read over the IEP carefully — numerous times. Numerous times, things discussed and agreed upon are written up differently in the IEP. IEP meetings move quickly, so you might read over the IEP and realize you need to remember something important.

3 APPROVE ONLY THE SECTIONS YOU WANT TO APPROVE.

If you only disagree with a portion of the IEP, you may sign the IEP and include a statement of exceptions to the items you disagree with. Those exceptions will not be implemented until the matter is resolved.

4 TAKE NOTES

As you read the IEP, write down your thoughts and objections. You can write a letter and add it as a supplement to the IEP. Having a day or two to reflect on the meeting after it's over can provide parents with clarity about whether the proposed IEP appropriately meets the needs of their child.

5 THE DISTRICT'S RESPONSE

The district will either have to incorporate your suggestions or provide you with prior written notice that explains why they don't believe they are legally required to include your requests.

Sample Email/Letter of IEP Concerns

Sometimes it is important to include a letter of concerns. Perhaps there were some concerns that weren't included, or a service or support that was agreed upon wasn't included on the written IEP.

Dear {school district case manager},

IThank you and the team for meeting today to discuss my child {name}. A lot of information was tossed around, so I want to ensure I have everything correct. As I recall, we discussed:

- Item of concern #1
- Item of concern #2
- Item of concern #3
- Try to keep the list short and simple.
- If you discussed something, but it was rejected list it again "we discussed a series of issues that seemed like they could only be addressed with a 1:1 aide, I realize most of the team disagreed with, but I still feel a 1:1 is the only real way to address the concerns."
- Also, list items you are unsure about. "There was a conversation about a social peers class. 12 weeks was mentioned in the IEP, but there isn't any information on when that class will begin, how long the sessions are, or how long it will go. Please include that information in the IEP."

Please let me know if I need to include anything or have misunderstood anything.

Sincerely,

Your Name

cc: your child's principal and your child's teacher(s)

THE SECRET
AUTISM ROADMAP

Implementing the IEP and Addressing School Concerns

"When a flower doesn't bloom you fix the environment in which it grows, not the flower."

— Shrinksdom

THE SECRET

Developing the IEP is exhausting, frustrating, and emotionally draining, but implementing the IEP is when the real work begins. One of the biggest problems is having different people working on goals differently. The speech therapist will be doing one thing. The occupational therapist will be doing another thing, and the teacher and special education teacher can do something completely different. You can only imagine how frustrating this if you also combine it with a home program doing things another way. Your job will be to unify the program. At times this can feel overwhelming, but it is extremely important for the success of your child's program.

Tips to Implementing the IEP

Connect With Your Child's Teacher(s) and Therapist(s)

Set up a time to meet privately with your child's teacher and find out what they need. Give them an overview of your child's strengths and challenges. Let them know how your current program works and what has been a success.

Create an IEP at a Glance

Modifications and accommodations should be remembered or avoided. A common complaint is teachers say they received so many modifications and accommodations, and they can't be expected to provide them all. Create an IEP at a Glance sheet. It should list accommodations, modifications, and tips to implement them.

Provide Tools to Help Teachers and Staff

If you use a reward system to incentivize or extinguish behaviors, let your child's teacher or Therapist know how it works and how they will be involved.

Establish an Easy, Reliable Communication System

It is essential to address issues before they become a real problem. The easiest way is to provide a quick communication system in a binder that goes back and forth daily.

For example:

- Johnny isn't eating his lunch.
- Janey earned stickers for good behavior in _____
- Billy had trouble with _____

Help Staff Help Your Child

No one knows better than you do how best to help your child stay calm and focused, manage difficult transitions, or interact with peers.

If you've already developed incredible ways to help your child manage behaviors at school, by all means, share them with your child's new teacher and staff.

For example:

- You may have created a terrific social story that helps your child remember to count to ten before exploding.
- Last year's teacher may have designed a tremendous visual schedule to help your child prepare for transitions.
- Your child's occupational therapist may have found the perfect sensory toy to help your child stay focused in class.
- Last year's aide may have developed phrases or ideas that helped your child say "yes" to social interactions.

Don't assume anyone from last year has shared anything with this year's group. Instead, be proactive and do it yourself!

Get Involved

Become a recess monitor or help out in the classroom helper occasionally. Teachers always appreciate the extra help, and you get invaluable observation time that can help during IEPs.

Spending time with teachers and staff is also very helpful in getting information on what behaviors you should be working on.

Connect Personally With Your Child's Teacher and Therapists

IEPs are contentious and emotional. It is easy to get angry, criticize, and yell at the IEP team, but when it is over, the real important work begins, and you don't want to burn bridges. After the IEP, you must build partnerships with your child's teacher, therapists, and aide. Good relationships can enhance the educational experience and contribute to the overall well-being and success of the child.

Establish a Communication System

A good relationship encourages open and frequent communication between parents and educators. Good communication allows for the quick and extremely important exchange of information, updates on progress, and discussions about strategies that work best for your child. It ensures that everyone involved is on the same page and can work in the same way with the same process.

Setting up a communication binder with your child's school can be a helpful way to facilitate effective communication and ensure that important information is shared between you, your child, and the school staff. You can divide the binder into sections using dividers or tabs and include a communication sheet that can be filled out by teachers or support staff on a daily or weekly basis

Advocacy

Developing a positive relationship with teachers and therapists empowers you to strongly advocate for your child and your child's teachers, therapists, and aide. It is very easy for IEPs to overload a teacher or special education teacher with too many goals. When you have a trusting and respectful relationship, you can communicate your concerns, ask questions, and voice the program's needs. When working collaboratively, you can ensure that your child receives all the necessary support and accommodations they require.

Your insights and perspectives as a parent are invaluable in helping educators tailor their instruction and interventions to effectively meet your child's individual needs. They will develop trust that you are ensuring a seamless transition and a cohesive approach to their assignments and your child's goals. When you establish a strong rapport, you become valued educational team members, working together to support your child's learning and development.

When a Teacher or Therapist Won't Communicate With You.

When faced with a teacher or therapist who won't communicate with you regarding your child, it can be challenging, but you can take steps to address the situation. Here are some suggestions:

- **INITIATE COMMUNICATION:** Reach out to the teacher or therapist and express your desire for open and regular communication. Send them a polite email or request a meeting to discuss your concerns.

- **DOCUMENT YOUR ATTEMPTS:** Record your attempts to communicate with the teacher or therapist. If the student is also exhibiting increased emotional outbursts or has suddenly become withdrawn, abuse could be involved, so make sure to document those instances.

- **CONSULT WITH THE PROGRAM COORDINATOR:** Reach out to the school's special education coordinator or case manager. They can act as a liaison and ensure communication channels are open.

- **CONSIDER A CHANGE:** Lack of communication is never a good sign. In cases where all attempts to improve communication have failed, you need to consider requesting a change of teacher or therapist.

- **INCLUDE COMMUNICATION IN YOUR IEP:** A strong communication system in your IEP can be very important in these situations. A child that lacks appropriate requires additional communication between the IEP team members.

Problems with the IEP

Suppose a school is not following the provisions outlined in a student's Individualized Education Plan, or there is a serious issue. In that case, several steps can be taken to resolve the issue:

- **REVIEW THE IEP:** Ensure that you clearly understand the provisions outlined in the IEP and what precisely is not being followed by the school.

- **COMMUNICATE WITH THE SCHOOL:** Discuss with the school staff and raise your concerns about the IEP not being followed. This may involve speaking with the teacher, special education coordinator, or school administrator.

- **DOCUMENT THE ISSUE(S):** Record instances where the school is not following the IEP, including dates, times, and a description.

- **REQUEST A MEETING WITH THE IEP TEAM:** You can ask to have a meeting with the IEP team to discuss your concerns and any disagreements you have with the IEP.

Next Steps

There are many times the school district will not want to budge. When that happens, the following steps can be:

- **SEEK OUTSIDE SUPPORT:** You can reach out to advocacy organizations or legal advocates for help in resolving the disagreement.

- **FILE A COMPLAINT:** If you have exhausted all other options, you can file a complaint with your state's Department of Education or with the Office for Civil Rights.

- **SEEK MEDIATION:** If the issue cannot be resolved through communication with the school or by filing a complaint, you may be able to participate in a mediation process with the school and a neutral third-party mediator.

- **CONSIDER LEGAL ACTION:** If the issue cannot be resolved through other means, you may need to consider taking legal action. An attorney experienced in special education law can guide this process.

It is important to remember that the IEP is a legally binding document, and schools must follow the provisions outlined in the plan. By resolving the issue, you can help ensure your child receives the special education services needed to succeed.

Document Everything

When school districts violate an IEP, they are violating special education law. It is important to start documenting because that will be used as evidence.

Letter to a Stranger

The purpose of a letter to a stranger is to imagine your letter being read by a complete stranger who knows nothing about the situation. Articulating the concerns, providing relevant information, and making specific requests can ensure that the letter effectively communicates your position.

Introduction

A brief introduction explaining the purpose of the letter, the child's name, and relevant background information.

Express Concerns or issues

A clear and concise description of the concerns or issues the writer wishes to address. This may include inadequate services, lack of accommodations, inappropriate placement, or failure to follow legal requirements.

Request for Action

A request for specific actions to be taken, such as a request for an evaluation, a meeting, or a request for changes to the child's IEP or placement.

Supporting Documentation

If applicable, the letter may include any relevant supporting documentation, such as medical reports, evaluations, or other records that help substantiate the concerns or arguments being made.

Contact Information

The letter should include the writer's contact information, such as a phone number or email address to facilitate further communication or follow-up.

Bullying is Not Tolerated

Bullying is not tolerated under the IDEA because it undermines the goals of providing a safe and inclusive educational environment for students with disabilities. Bullying has an adverse impact on educational progress. It creates a hostile environment that impedes a student's access to educational opportunities and denies them the benefits of a supportive learning environment.

Schools must use evidence-based bullying prevention and intervention programs. **SCHOOL DISTRICTS ARE MANDATED** to immediately address bullying by investigating to determine practical steps to address parent concerns and intervene on the student's behalf.

35%
of autistic children experiences bullying

20%
of children with learning disabilities experiences bullying

Types of Bullying

Bullying comes in many forms. It can be physical bullying, verbal insults, harassment, or social bullying. Cyberbullying adds the component of making bullying widely "public" via social media. Bullying can cause emotional distress, social isolation, and a decline in academic performance, directly contradicting the goal of providing a FAPE.

Detrimental Effects of Bullying

Bullying adversely affects children in many ways. Some of these are:

- Physical injury
- School avoidance/School refusal
- Increased anxiety or depression
- Self-harm/self-injurious behaviors
- Decrease in academic performance evidenced by a lack of progress or regression
- Loss of self-esteem
- Excessive truancies
- Increased drop-out rates
- Suicidal ideology or suicide

Reporting Bullying

Parents and students need to report incidents of bullying promptly. If a school fails to appropriately respond to bullying incidents, parents can contact the school administration, the district's special education coordinator, or local education authorities to seek further assistance and support.

Why Do Schools Downplay Bullying?

Even though addressing bullying is mandated, teachers often ignore bullying, and schools often try to downplay bullying. Teachers and administrators often don't know much about bullying or what to do, even if they have a strict rule against bullying, so they just don't report it. School authorities also feel that reporting such instances might harm the reputation of their school. In some cases, they feel that the kids should deal with it on their own, or they will ask them to shake hands.

How a School Should Handle Bullying.

- **ESTABLISH CLEAR POLICIES AND PROCEDURES:** Schools should have clear, comprehensive anti-bullying policies that outline expectations for behavior define bullying, and describe the consequences.

- **PROVIDE TRAINING AND AWARENESS:** School staff, including teachers, administrators, and support personnel, should receive training on recognizing, preventing, and addressing bullying effectively. Students should also receive age-appropriate education and awareness programs to promote a culture of respect, empathy, and inclusivity.

- **PROMPTLY RESPOND TO REPORTS OF BULLYING:** School staff should conduct thorough investigations, documenting incidents, and taking necessary disciplinary actions.

- **PROVIDE SUPPORT TO VICTIMS AND PERPETRATORS:** Victims may require counseling, additional support, or accommodations to help them recover.

Students with disabilities have additional protections.

Bullying of a student based on his or her disability may result in a disability-based harassment violation. If families are having problems with bullying of their child with special needs, they should bring their concerns to the administration by writing a letter to the Special Education Director, Superintendent, and School Board.

Compensatory Education

Compensatory education refers to additional educational services or supports provided to students with disabilities to make up for any educational opportunities they may have missed or been denied. It is a remedy to compensate for any loss of learning or progress caused by a school's failure to provide the appropriate services and supports outlined in a student's IEP.

Services Were Not Provided

If a school fails to provide the services, accommodations, or related supports outlined in a student's IEP, resulting in the student being deprived of their educational rights, compensatory education may be considered.

Extended Delays or Disruptions

If extended delays or disruptions in the provision of services significantly impact the student's educational progress, compensatory education may be appropriate. This could occur, for example, when a student experiences a long-term absence of necessary special education services or an extended interruption in their education due to circumstances beyond their control.

Inadequate Progress

If a student with a disability is not making expected progress due to the school's failure to implement the IEP appropriately, compensatory education can be considered a means to make up for the lack of progress.

It is quite common for school districts to not provide numerous days of agreed-upon therapy. A therapist or aide might be out sick, but occasionally there might not be a therapist or aide or they have been assigned other duties. It is crucial to make the school district aware they are not providing the agreed-upon services outlined in the IEP. Still, even then the amount and nature of compensatory education may vary depending on the specific circumstances of the case, including the nature and extent of the educational harm or loss suffered by the student. If you believe that your child may be eligible for compensatory education, it is advisable to consult with a special education advocate or attorney who can provide guidance based on your specific circumstances. There are also time limits on when compensatory education claims end.

School Refusal

School refusal, also known as school avoidance or school phobia, refers to a child's persistent reluctance or refusal to attend school. It is a complex issue that can stem from various factors and significantly impact a child's well-being and educational progress. Here's how school refusal can affect a child:

EMOTIONAL DISTRESS

Children experiencing school refusal often experience intense emotional distress, such as anxiety, fear, or depression. The thought of going to school may trigger feelings of panic or unease.

ACADEMIC CHALLENGES

Consistent school avoidance can result in significant disruptions to a child's education. Missed school can lead to falling behind academically, difficulty keeping up with coursework, and gaps in learning.

SOCIAL ISOLATION

School refusal can lead to social isolation for the child. Missing school means missing out on social interactions, peer relationships, and opportunities for social skill development.

IMPACT ON FAMILY

School refusal can place a burden on the child's family. Parents may experience stress, frustration, and concern for their child's well-being and education.

LIMITS EDUCATION

School refusal can limit a child's access to educational opportunities and experiences. They may miss out on specialized programs, which can have long-term implications for their personal and academic growth.

LONG-TERM CONSEQUENCES

If left unaddressed, school refusal can have long-term consequences. It can impact a child's educational trajectory, career opportunities, and overall life outcomes.

Addressing school refusal requires a comprehensive and collaborative approach. Strategies may include understanding and addressing the underlying causes of the unwillingness, implementing accommodations or supports, and providing social emotional interventions to help manage anxiety or other emotional challenges.

School Discipline

If a child with a disability exhibits behaviors that are addressed in their IEP and they are punished for those behaviors, it may be considered a violation of their rights under the Individuals with Disabilities Education Act (IDEA) or other relevant laws, such as Section 504 of the Rehabilitation Act of 1973. These laws protect students with disabilities from discrimination and ensure they receive a free and appropriate public education.

These situations are obvious failures of the behavior intervention program. Parents or guardians need to advocate for their child's rights and work collaboratively with the school. Here are some steps that can be taken:

- **REVIEW THE IEP:** Parents should carefully review the child's IEP to ensure that the behaviors for which the child is being punished are addressed in the plan. The IEP should include strategies, supports, and interventions to address the child's unique needs.

- **COMMUNICATE WITH THE SCHOOL:** Punishments go on a child's permanent record, so parents need to address with written documentation and contest the punishment. It is essential to emphasize the punishment is being emposed because of the child's disability.

- **PROVIDE DOCUMENTATION:** Parents can provide documentation, such as reports from professionals who have evaluated the child, to support their claim that the behaviors are related to the disability and require specific interventions. This can help demonstrate the need for improved accommodations and supports instead of punitive measures.

- **REQUEST AN IEP MEETING:** If the child's IEP needs to be revised to address the behaviors in question more effectively, parents can request an IEP meeting. If the current program is ineffective, this can be a primary reason to replace the current program with a more effective program.

- **SEEK ASSISTANCE FROM ADVOCACY ORGANIZATIONS:** If the school is unresponsive or if the situation becomes more contentious, parents can reach out to local or national advocacy organizations specializing in disability rights. These organizations can provide guidance, support, and legal advice on how to proceed.

Use of Negative Reinforcements

If a school district proposes negative reinforcement or punishment to address behaviors related to a child's disability, it is important to approach the situation carefully. In some states, punishment includes restraints, physical takedowns, and seclusion rooms. Negative reinforcement and punishment can have unintended consequences and are not an effective approach to addressing behavioral concerns. Here are some steps you can take:

- **REVIEW THE IEP:** Carefully review the child's IEP to ensure that the proposed negative reinforcement are not included in the IEP. The IEP needs to prioritize positive behavior supports, accommodations, and interventions that promote the child's learning and well-being.

- **ADVOCATE FOR POSITIVE BEHAVIOR SUPPORTS:** Engage in a dialogue with the school district to advocate for the using positive behavior supports and interventions that are research-based, evidence-based, and aligned with best practices in special education. Positive behavior supports focus on teaching and reinforcing appropriate behaviors rather than solely relying on punishments.

- **REQUEST A MEETING:** Document your refusal for punishments or negative consequences. You can also provide articles, research or evidence supporting the effectiveness of positive approaches in addressing the child's specific behaviors.

- **SEEK EXPERT OPINIONS:** If necessary, seek input from professionals with expertise in special education, behavior analysis, or related fields. They can provide additional insights and recommendations that support the use of positive behavior supports and help counter-arguments in favor of punishment.

- **COLLABORATE WITH OTHER PARENTS:** Reach out to other parents of students with disabilities within the school district who may have faced similar situations. Collaborate with them to raise awareness, share information, and advocate collectively for positive behavior supports and appropriate interventions.

- **INVOLVE ADVOCACY ORGANIZATIONS:** Contact local or national advocacy organizations focusing on disability rights and special education. They can provide guidance, resources, and support in navigating the situation and advocating for the child's rights.

- **CONSIDER LEGAL ASSISTANCE:** If all attempts to resolve the situation amicably are unsuccessful, you may want to consult with an attorney specializing in education law. They can help assess the situation, provide legal advice, and determine if further action, such as filing a complaint, is necessary.

Stay Involved

There are several ways you can become involved in your child's school and actively participate in your child's education. Here are some suggestions:

These situations are obvious failures of the behavior intervention program. It is important for parents or guardians to advocate for their child's rights and work collaboratively with the school. Here are some steps that can be taken:

- **ATTEND PARENT-TEACHER CONFERENCES:** Make it a priority to attend parent-teacher conferences to meet your child's teachers, discuss their progress, and gain insights into their academic and social development. These meetings provide an opportunity for open communication and collaboration with the school.

- **JOIN THE PARENT-TEACHER ASSOCIATION (PTA) OR PARENT-TEACHER ORGANIZATION (PTO):** Get involved with the PTA or PTO at your child's school. These organizations often coordinate various activities and events, such as fundraisers, family nights, and educational programs. They also provide a platform to connect with other parents and contribute to school initiatives.

- **VOLUNTEER IN THE CLASSROOM:** Contact your child's teacher and inquire about volunteer opportunities in the classroom. You could help with tasks like reading to students, organizing materials, or assisting with special projects. Volunteering allows you to actively engage with your child's learning environment and build a connection with their teacher.

- **ATTEND SCHOOL EVENTS AND ACTIVITIES:** Attend school events, such as performances, sports competitions, and parent workshops. These events provide opportunities to meet other parents, engage with the school community, and better understand your child's school life beyond the classroom.

- **STAY INFORMED:** Stay updated on school news, policies, and important announcements by regularly checking the school's website, newsletters, or social media channels. This keeps you informed about school events, changes, and opportunities to get involved.

- **ATTEND SCHOOL BOARD MEETINGS:** School board meetings are official gatherings of the school board members, typically held at regular intervals. These meetings serve as a platform for board members to discuss and make decisions regarding the school district's operation, policies, and governance. There is also a time when people can make statements or express concerns to the school board.

The School Board

You can change processes on the School Board. A school board is a governing body responsible for overseeing and making decisions regarding the operation and policies of a school district. The superintendent and school district personnel answer directly to the school board. In some districts, getting on the School Board is very easy. You will need to sign up and run a campaign in other school districts.

Here are some key functions typically associated with school boards:

- **POLICY DEVELOPMENT:** School boards develop, review, and adopt policies that guide the overall operation of the school district.

- **BUDGET OVERSIGHT:** School boards approve the district's budget, which includes allocating funds for various educational programs, staffing, facilities, and resources.

- **SUPERINTENDENT EVALUATION AND SELECTION:** School boards hire and evaluate the superintendent. They set performance goals, provide feedback, and may make decisions about contract renewals or terminations.

- **CURRICULUM AND INSTRUCTION:** School boards collaborate with educators and administrators to establish educational goals.

- **COMMUNITY ENGAGEMENT:** School boards act as a link between the school district and the community. They engage with parents, students, teachers, and community members to gather input, address concerns, and communicate important information about district policies, initiatives, and events.

- **ADVOCACY AND POLICY ADHERENCE:** School boards advocate for the needs and interests of students and the district. They ensure compliance with legal and regulatory requirements, such as education laws, state mandates, and federal guidelines.

- **HIRING AND PERSONNEL DECISIONS:** School boards participate in selecting and hiring key personnel, such as principals and administrators.

THE SECRET
AUTISM ROADMAP

IEP Breakdowns

"Families in the special needs system often face a constant battle for access to services and support, leaving them exhausted and frustrated."

— *Author Unknown*

THE SECRET

A parent's relationship with a school district can break down or be broken before it even starts, leading to escalating conflicts and tension. Many school districts don't like working with special needs children or families. This becomes evident when communication between parents and the school district becomes strained, and attempts at resolving the issues through meetings and discussions prove unfruitful. The situation can escalate into an adversarial environment. As frustrations mount and trust erodes, it may seem the only way to protect the child's rights and ensure an appropriate education is through legal solutions.

When the school district shuts you out, proceeding to legal solutions, such as due process hearings or filing complaints with the appropriate education authorities, may become necessary to resolve issues. Legal avenues can provide parents with a formal mechanism to assert their child's rights, seek enforcement, and provide a safe place for education. While legal actions should always be seen as a last resort, they can sometimes be the only way to ensure that the school district fulfills its obligations and supports the child's educational needs. Engaging in legal proceedings can be emotionally challenging, costly, and time-consuming. Still, it may be the most effective way to address the breakdown in the parent-school relationship and secure a positive educational outcome for the child.

IEP Relationship Breakdowns

It is very common for school district relationships with the parents to break down. IEPs are contentious and emotional. The most common complaint is that parents don't feel the school's program is doing enough, and school personnel feel they are being asked to do too much. In a recent 60 Minutes segment, a series of teachers complained they aren't able to teach a class with special needs students in the class. They didn't include that it was their employer, the school district, that wasn't providing adequate support for the teacher. You can see how the breakdown starts. School districts often feel you should be happy with what they offer, or if they give your child a particular program to meet their needs, they will need to provide other children with a particular program. There could also be a school district defending a lousy staff member, or if you want to get a better program, they will make you jump through some legal hoops. There are many reasons why IEP breakdowns happen:

EXPECTATIONS
School districts often feel they only need to provide minimal results and no more.

COMMUNICATION ISSUES
As a school's program struggles communication gets harder and more strained.

GOALS AND SERVICES
Parents often feel the IEP goals are not ambitious enough, or that the services provided are insufficient.

IMPLEMENTATION ISSUES
School districts often over-promise on their services and underdeliver on their delivery.

PARENTAL CONCERNS
Parents often feel that their input or concerns are not being valued or taken into consideration.

PROCEDURAL ISSUES
School districts regularly violate special education law with little to no repercussions.

ADVOCACY FATIGUE
Advocacy efforts often cause stress which makes it challenging to maintain positive relationships.

DIFFICULT TO WORK WITH
Some school districts are just difficult to work with. It could be personal or just general policy.

Special Needs Advocate

The IEP process is extremely confusing and making sure the IEP gets implemented is even more challenging. In those cases, the assistance of a special education advocate can facilitate constructive dialogue and resolution of conflicts.

- **EXPERTISE AND KNOWLEDGE:** Special education advocates understand the laws, regulations, and procedures related to special education services and can help parents navigate the complex system.

- **ENSURING APPROPRIATE SERVICES:** An advocate can help ensure that a child has the necessary goals, accommodations, modifications, and support services.

- **UNDERSTAND THE CHILD, THEIR RIGHTS, AND ENTITLEMENTS:** They can inform parents about their child's needs and rights and help them assert them.

- **COLLABORATION AND COMMUNICATION:** They can help parents articulate their concerns and work towards developing appropriate educational plans. They understand where you can compromise and where you need to negotiate.

- **MEDIATION AND CONFLICT RESOLUTION:** Advocates understanding the law differs from quoting the law and can facilitate negotiations, provide objective perspectives, and work towards finding acceptable solutions.

- **SUPPORT DURING MEETINGS AND EVALUATIONS:** They can provide emotional support, clarify information, and ensure that parents' concerns are addressed.

- **TIME AND RESOURCE MANAGEMENT:** Advocates can help parents manage paperwork, deadlines and gather relevant documentation.

- **SELF-ADVOCACY:** Advocates can empower parents to understand the special education process, ask informed questions, and participate in decision-making.

Tips to Hiring a Special Needs Advoate

Call several experienced special needs attorneys and ask for a referral. They usually know the experienced advocates and can steer you in the right direction. Some attorneys employ advocates in their firms. Some good questions to ask when interviewing special needs advocates are:

- Ask for referrals and check their credentials.

- Ask if they have observed or represented a parent in a due process hearing.

- Check the advocate's fees. Some advocates charge as much as a skilled attorney.

How to Handle IEP Disagreements

Quite often, there are disagreements with the IEP. School Districts have gone to great lengths and excelled at creating what is called defensible programs. A defensible program is a special education program that is legally and educationally sound — on paper. The program has an official-sounding name and sounds excellent. At first glance, it appears to meet the student's unique needs to the greatest extent possible, but in reality, the program is nothing like how it was described and fails in its reach and scope.

When programs are offered, it is imperative to request a detailed discussion of that program and then request to observe it. In most cases, just asking a few questions shows that the program doesn't follow evidence-based procedures. When these happen, it is crucial to document why you feel the school district's program will be ineffective.

Document Your Concerns

School districts will often overstate their abilities. They might put too much on a teacher who doesn't have the time. They often overstate the ability of their program, or their evaluation won't fully address your child's deficits. Make your concerns known. Write them out and have them included with the IEP. Send a follow-up email and most importantly, when things do wrong, inform the school and request they provide the service they promised.

Record IEP Meetings

School districts often describe a great program, but then the parents will find out later that the program doesn't match the description. Occasional programs are suggested but then not included in the written IEP. IEP recording can quickly resolve these issues.

School Retaliation

When a school district's programs begin to struggle or show signs of failure, a parent will begin to ask questions or complain. It isn't uncommon for schools to respond with retaliation. As a response, the school district might start implementing new rules and restrictions. They might tell you to stop dropping off your child in front of their classroom and instead wait off campus even when other parents are allowed to drop off their child in front of their classroom. The level of support for your child might drop off. Quite often, communication with school staff might become very limited or completely stop. These are signs of retaliation.

Getting School DIstricts Upset

School districts are made up of people at the administration level. Occasionally those people can become very petty. Perhaps they don't want their school district to get a reputation for providing special education services. Some might not feel their teachers should have to deal with special education students. Either way, there have been many cases where school districts decide to make some special education families' lives much more difficult. Some examples include:

The school district might call CPS on the family.

- Access to your child's class will be limited.

- The school will discipline your child in any way.

- The school may spread false, derogatory information about you.

- A teacher can retaliate against a targeted student by being hostile towards them, ignoring them or being dismissive.

- Siblings will also experience discrimination by not making sports teams or being chosen for theater roles, and such

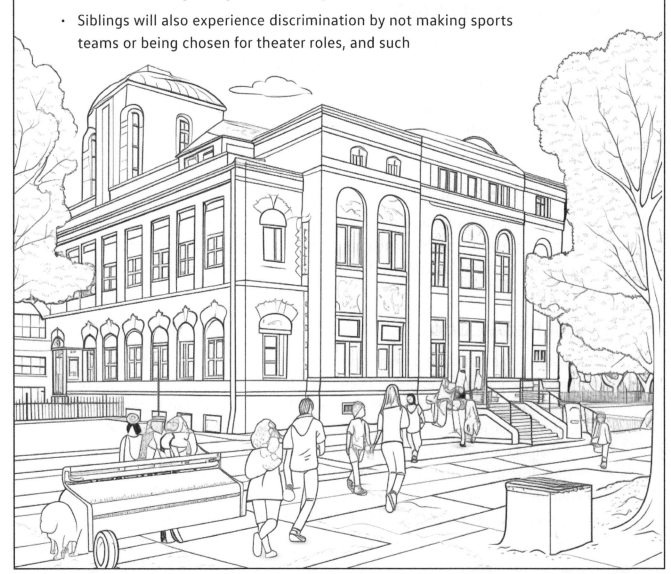

Definition of Retaliation

The Office of Civil Rights has clearly defined retaliation and has a 5-part test to help determine if a family has experienced it.

OCR Definition of Retaliation

Parents need to show the following to prove their case:

- Has the student/parent engaged in a protected activity? (such as advocacy)

- Is the district aware of the protected activity?

- Was the parent/student subjected to an adverse action?

- Will a neutral third party decide there is a causal relationship or connection between the protected activity and the adverse reaction?

- Can the district offer legitimate, nondiscriminatory reasons for the adverse action, which a neutral third party will not consider to be pretextual (i.e., a false pretense)?

Retaliation claims must be strictly alleged and meet the evidentiary standard to be successful.

Retaliation claims must be strictly alleged and meet the evidentiary standard to be successful. Retaliatory action is defined broadly. "The law deliberately does not take a 'laundry list' approach to retaliation because, unfortunately, its forms are as varied as the human imagination will permit."

Rebuffing parent involvement is a subtle form of retaliation that is not easy to discern. For this reason, parent participation in the decision-making process regarding a child's educational program is a significant procedural right under the Individuals with Disabilities Education Act (IDEA). The purpose of legislating the role of parents in a child's special education program is explicitly to "balance the natural advantage of districts."

To state a case of retaliation under the ADA and section 504, an individual must show that (1) they engaged in a protected activity, (2) they suffered an adverse action, and (3) there was a causal link between the two.

The adverse action must be causally related to the protected activity, and the rationale provided for the adverse action as a pretext is the most challenging aspect of a retaliation claim. If the plaintiff establishes a case of retaliation, the burden shifts to the defendant to show a legitimate, nonretaliatory purpose for its actions.

Resolving Disputes

When the IEP isn't working for the school district or parents, there are additional ways to resolve disputes.

IEP Facilitation

IEP facilitation aims to foster open communication, mutual understanding, and consensus-building among all participants. The facilitator helps guide the IEP meeting, ensures everyone's perspectives are heard, and promotes a constructive problem-solving environment.

Mediation

IEP mediation is a voluntary process to resolve disputes between parents and school districts regarding developing, implementing, or revising an Individualized Education Program (IEP) for a student with special needs. It involves the assistance of a neutral and trained mediator who facilitates communication and negotiation between the parties involved. The mediator helps identify the issues in dispute, encourages open dialogue, and assists in generating potential solutions.

Alternative Dispute Resolution

Due process ADR aims to promote a less adversarial and more collaborative environment, encourage meaningful participation from all parties, and ultimately find a resolution that meets the student's educational needs while avoiding the formalities and potential costs of a due process hearing.

Compliance Complaint

This type of complaint typically asserts that the school district has not implemented or provided the services, accommodations, or supports outlined in the student's IEP, thereby denying the student the educational benefits they are entitled to receive.

Due Process Complaint

A due process complaint is a formal complaint filed by a parent or guardian to initiate a due process hearing to resolve disputes related to the identification, evaluation, educational placement, or provision of services for a student with special needs.

IEP Facilitation

There are times when an IEP team has trouble communicating and solving problems collaboratively solving problems there might be an opportunity to have a mediator facilitate the meeting. This can be done through SELPA, school districts, or the state's Department of Education. A facilitator isn't available in all states. When a facilitator is provided, they are provided at no cost to the school district or parent.

- The family and the school must agree to have a facilitator.

- The facilitator will try to guide the discussion and facilitate the meeting to the benefit of the student with workable solutions.

- The facilitator tries to keep the IEP team on task and ensure the decisions are included in the IEP.

When Should You Hire a Special Needs Attorney

Hiring a special needs attorney is necessary in certain situations. Special needs attorneys rarely get involved in Special Education Law for the money. But instead, because it is often personal. Hiring an attorney can be expensive but necessary in certain situations. Legal expertise and representation are often required in these situations:

- **DISPUTES WITH THE SCHOOL DISTRICT**
  If you are involved in a disagreement or dispute with your child's school district regarding special education services, an attorney can provide legal guidance and advocacy. This may include disputes over the appropriateness of services, eligibility determinations, IEP development, or legal rights violations. It is a good idea to arrange a free consultation, with a few special education attorneys, and listen to what they feel would be the best way to proceed.

- **DUE PROCESS PROCEEDINGS**
  If you need to initiate or respond to a due process complaint or due process hearing a special needs attorney can represent your interests, prepare your case, and navigate the legal process.

- **DISCRIMINATION OR CIVIL RIGHTS VIOLATIONS:** In cases where you suspect your child has experienced discrimination or civil rights violations related to their disability a special needs attorney can help you understand your legal rights and pursue appropriate actions to help address the situation.

Before you Hire a Special Education Attorney

Special education lawyers work to ensure that children with disabilities receive the education they are entitled to and that their rights are protected. Still, they are not miracle workers and are very expensive. They require you to do the prep work.

GATHER STRONG EVIDENCE
Parents need to gather and organize strong evidence to support their case. This primarily includes the parents expressing their concerns in correspondence and any other relevant documentation demonstrating the child's needs and the district's failure to meet them.

CONSULT WITH ATTORNIES AND BUILD A STRONG CASE
Often people want to go to Due Process listing only procedural violations during an IEP. That is a sign the school district doesn't respect special education law, but most hearing officers don't put that much weight into those issues. Focus on more significant issues of failing programs that the school refuses to address or the school refusing to provide services. A great idea to consult with a few Special Needs Attornies and look for the best way to proceed.

DON'T WAIT UNTIL THE LAST MINUTE
If you are having trouble with your school district, it is a good idea to meet with some special education attornies and put one on retainer. See if you can work out a deal on price. In most cases, when the school district finds out you have an attorney, they will think twice about how to address your program.

LIMIT ATTORNEY FEES
School districts understand attorneys are expensive and will try to abuse that by only communicating through your attorney. This can become very expensive, so it is crucial to sign an agreement with the attorney that limits their communication with a school district until after a case is filed.

Mediation

Mediation might be an appropriate or alternative dispute resolution option when the school district and family are at an impasse and can't come to an agreement. Mediation is a dispute resolution process that uses a trained person to assist the school district and parents in agreeing to resolve their conflict or dispute. Unlike a judge or arbitrator, the mediator does not decide the outcome of the dispute.

- **WHAT IS A MEDIATION:** Mediation is a voluntary process that brings people together with a mediator, who helps them communicate with each other and resolve their disagreements. The mediator is conducted by someone who has completed a mediation training course and some additional training. You can request the training, experience, and background of the mediator. You can also request the experience or knowledge in mediating your dispute type. Mediators are chosen on a rotating basis. Neither the parents nor the school district can pick a mediator alone.

- **WHAT IS THE MEDIATOR'S JOB:** Helps participants develop ground rules for the session and creates a safe environment that encourages participants to respect other points of view. They will guide the discussion by listening, identifying interests, and clarifying concerns. The mediator is knowledgeable of laws relating to special education but does not make decisions.

- **WHEN IS THIS USED:** When there is a disagreement between parents and educators about special education and related services.

- **WHO INITIATES:** A parent or school district may request mediation. Mediation is voluntary, so the parent and school district must agree to participate. There is no cost to the school district or parents. The mediator and facilities are provided at public expense.

- **WHAT IS THE OUTCOME:** Whether there is a resolution of the issues or an agreement is created, depends upon the participants. Complex situations may require multiple mediation sessions to come to agreement. There is no guarantee that a written agreement will be created. Parents and school educators must both agree to participate. Mediation discussions are confidential. Mediation agreements must be in writing

Alternative Dispute Resolution

A resolution meeting takes place after a parent or school district files a due process complaint/hearing request but before a due process hearing takes place.

- **WHAT IS A RESOLUTION MEETING:** A resolution meeting provides the parent and school district a chance to work together to resolve issues before a due process hearing. Keeps decision-making with the parent and school district who know the child. The school district may only bring an attorney to the resolution meeting if the parent chooses to bring an attorney. The parent or school district may cancel a resolution agreement within three business days. Discussions at the resolution meeting are not confidential, and you cannot be required to sign a confidentiality form to participate in the meeting. Parents and the school district may choose to sign a confidentiality agreement or include it in a resolution agreement.

- **TIMEFRAME:** The school district must hold a resolution meeting within 15 calendar days of receiving notice of a parent's due process complaint/hearing request. A parent may ask the hearing officer or administrative law judge to start the hearing timeline if the school district does not hold the resolution meeting on time. The parties have up to 30 calendar days to work on a resolution prior to the hearing timeline. The hearing officer or administrative law judge may extend this period at the parties' request.

- **WHAT IS THE OUTCOME:** Resolution meetings allow parents and school districts to resolve issues without going to a hearing. There is no cost to the parents – the meeting is provided at public expense.

Compliance Complaint

A compliance complaint is typically filed when a school district has not complied with a special education law or procedure. When a school district violates part or all of a special education law or procedure, parents can file a complaint with your state's Department of Education. These violations include, but are not limited to:

- failure to provide parents with their child's educational records within 5 days of their request;
- failure to implement parts or all of an IEP
- failure to follow timelines for an assessment
- failure to implement a due process or mediation agreement

- **WHAT IS A COMPLIANCE COMPLAINT:** A compliance complaint is a written document communicating how your school district has not followed IDEA and requesting an investigation. You can contact your state's Department of Education to find out the specifics about their procedures for filing a compliance complaint. They should be able to provide you with the necessary information and guidance.

- **TIMELINE:** A written decision must be issued no later than 60 calendar days after receiving the complaint unless the timeline is extended. A written state complaint is relatively easy to file.

- **WHAT IS THE INVESTIGATOR'S JOB:** When filing the complaint, provide a a detailed account of the issues, including the specific aspects of the IEP that are not being implemented correctly or any special education violations. Include supporting documentation, such as evaluations, progress reports, correspondence, or other relevant records. The state is responsible for ensuring that an investigation is done, if necessary, and a decision is made about the complaint. An investigator will review information related to the complaint. They may interview or meet with people related to the complaint. They will make findings and a determination based on applicable law.

- **WHEN IS THIS USED:** This is available anytime there is a concern about a particular child or an issue that affects children system-wide.

- **WHO INITIATES:** Any person or organization may file a written state complaint. This is the only dispute resolution option open to any person or organization, including those unrelated to the child. The final decision may include child-specific corrective actions or related to system-wide issues. The person or organization filing the complaint must provide facts to support the problems listed in their complaint. This process does not require those involved to try resolving the dispute collaboratively. Mediation remains available anytime. The investigation and decision are provided at public expense at no cost to the complainant. The IDEA does not require states to offer an appeal process for the written decision— check with your state educational agency for options that may be available.

- **WHAT IS THE OUTCOME:** A written decision includes findings and conclusions and lists reasons for the final decision. It must also include actions required to address the needs of the child or children related to the complaint.

WITHDRAWING COMPLAINTS: There are times you may want to withdraw your complaint. If the investigator disagrees with your complaint, you may be unable to ask for a due process hearing on the same issue. Also, if you find that the investigator who received your complaint is "school friendly." Or if they are concerned there currently is not enough evidence.

Due Process Complaint

Filing for Due Process is a formal legal procedure typically initiated when there is a severe dispute between parents and the school district regarding FAPE. Due process is used to resolve disagreements relating to the identification, evaluation, educational placement, or provision of a free, appropriate public education to a child who needs or is suspected of needing special education and related services.

- **SEEK LEGAL ADVICE:** Due process complaints involve complex legal procedures. It is advisable to consult with an attorney who specializes in special education law. A parent or school district may file a due process complaint/hearing request.

- **DOCUMENT THE CONCERNS:** It is essential to document your issues with the IEP or the provision of special education services. This will serve as evidence to support your complaint.

- **TIMELINE:** Under IDEA, due process complaints must be filed within 2 years of the date when a party knew or should have known of the problem. The written decision must be issued within 45 calendar days from the end of the resolution period unless a party requests a specific extension of the timeline.

- **PREPARE THE DUE PROCESS COMPLAINT:** Work with your attorney, if you have one, to draft the due process complaint. Include a detailed description of the issues, the specific violations of law or regulations, and the requested relief or resolution. Ensure you meet all the requirements specified by your jurisdiction and the school district. From the date the complaint is filed until the decision is final, your child stays in their current educational placement unless you and the school district agree otherwise – this is called "pendency" or "stay-put."

- **COSTS:** The hearing, hearing officer, or administrative law judge, facilities, and decision are provided at public expense, but each party pays its expenses, which may include attorneys' fees and witnesses. Attorney costs and prices used to be included in decisions, but hearing officers have been reducing those fees.

- **ROLE OF THE HEARING OFFICER:** The hearing officer or administrative law judge oversees the hearing timeline, including all pre-hearing activities. The conducts the hearing and manages procedural matters. They use applicable law to write a decision based on evidence and testimony presented at the hearing. They may dismiss the complaint if the issues are resolved before the hearing.

PARTICIPATE IN RESOLUTION PROCESSES: After filing the due process complaint, your jurisdiction may require alternative dispute resolution (ADR) options such as mediation or a resolution meeting. ADR is a type of dispute resolution that is cheaper and faster than traditional legal options. A mediator manages them to provide an opportunity to resolve the dispute without going through a formal hearing. Mediation is voluntary. If the mediation is held, the parties will reach an agreement, or they won't. Once the mediation is held, OAH will close the case. If the parties do not reach an agreement, the party requesting the mediation can file a due process complaint by filing a new action.

- **ATTEND THE DUE PROCESS HEARING:** If the dispute remains unresolved through ADR or if you opt not to engage in ADR, a due process hearing may be scheduled. This is a formal legal proceeding where both parties present their arguments and evidence before an impartial hearing officer or administrative law judge. Be prepared to present your case and support your claims with evidence and witnesses.

- **WHAT IS THE OUTCOME:** Following the due process hearing, the hearing officer or administrative law judge will issue a written decision. Review the decision carefully and consider your options for further action, such as appealing the decision if you disagree with the outcome.

Expedited Hearing Request

An expedited due process hearing is a particular type of due process hearing which may be requested only in certain situations that relate to discipline and disagreement with the educational placement of a student with a disability.

- A resolution meeting must occur within 7 calendar days unless the parties agree in writing not to have the meeting or use mediation instead.

- The hearing proceeds if the issue is not resolved within 15 calendar days.

- The hearing must be held within 20 school days of the request being filed.

- The decision must be issued within 10 school days of the hearing.

Special Education Legal Resources

Legal resources can provide valuable information on special education. Often special education attorneys are available for a free consultation. These resources can provide information and support related to special education laws:

- **OFFICE OF SPECIAL EDUCATION PROGRAMS (OSEP):** Their website offers access to federal laws and regulations, policy guidance, and publications.

- **INDIVIDUALS WITH DISABILITIES EDUCATION ACT (IDEA) WEBSITE:** The IDEA website provides comprehensive information about federal law, regulations, guidance documents, and resources for parents and educators.

- **COUNCIL OF PARENT ATTORNEYS AND ADVOCATES (COPAA):** Their website offers resources, training, and information on legal issues related to special education, including guidance on IEPs, dispute resolution, and strategies.

- **WRIGHTSLAW:** Wrightslaw is a popular online resource dedicated to special education law and advocacy. Their website provides articles, books, training materials, and a vast collection of resources on various legal topics, including IEPs, evaluation and eligibility, dispute resolution, and procedural safeguards.

- **DISABILITY RIGHTS EDUCATION & DEFENSE FUND (DREDF):** DREDF is a national law and policy center dedicated to protecting and advancing the rights of people with disabilities.

- **NATIONAL CENTER FOR LEARNING DISABILITIES (NCLD):** NCLD is an organization that provides information, resources, and support for individuals with learning disabilities and their families.

- **NATIONAL DISABILITY RIGHTS NETWORK (NDRN):** Their website provides information on special education law, including fact sheets, publications, and resources related to advocacy and dispute resolution.

- **SPECIAL EDUCATION LAW BLOGS:** There are several legal blogs dedicated to special education law, such as "Special Education Law Blog" by Charles P. Fox, "The Wrightslaw Way" by Peter W. D. Wright and Pamela Darr Wright, and "IDEA Legal Blog" by Mark C. Weber.

- **STATE EDUCATION AGENCIES:** Each state has its education agency responsible for implementing and overseeing special education services.

- **LOCAL PARENT TRAINING AND INFORMATION CENTERS (PTIS):** PTIs are federally funded centers that provide training and resources to parents of children with disabilities. They often offer assistance with understanding special education laws and regulations, navigating the IEP process, and providing advocacy support.

Office of Administrative Hearings (OAH)

The Office of Administrative Hearings (OAH) is an independent agency in several states within the United States. The OAH is responsible for conducting administrative hearings and resolving disputes in various areas, including special education. The name of the OAH may vary per state.

Are you curious about what special education decisions are being decided in your community? You can look up the Office of Administrative Special Education (OAH)

- **DETERMINE THE JURISDICTION:** OAH decisions are specific to a particular jurisdiction, typically at the state level. Identify the state where the hearing decision you are interested in taking place.

- **VISIT THE APPROPRIATE OAH WEBSITE:** Each state has its own OAH or similar administrative hearing body that handles special education disputes. Visit the website of the OAH for the relevant state.

- **NAVIGATE TO THE SPECIAL EDUCATION SECTION:** Once on the OAH website, look for a section or tab related to special education or special education hearings. This section may provide information on hearing decisions or links to access them.

- **SEARCH FOR HEARING DECISIONS:** Within the special education section, there may be a search function or a list of available hearing decisions. Use the provided search tools to find specific decisions by entering relevant keywords, such as the names of the parties involved, the date of the decision, or the case number.

- **REVIEW THE AVAILABLE DECISIONS:** Browse through the search results or list of available decisions to find the specific case or topic you are interested in. The decisions are typically presented in a downloadable format, such as PDF files.

- **ACCESS THE DECISION:** Click on the relevant decision to access the full text. The decision may include details about the case, the arguments presented by both sides, the administrative law judge's findings, and the dispute's outcome or resolution.

Nondisclosure Agrrements

Over 70% of Due Process Complaints are resolved in Alternative Dispute Resolution or Mediation. Those decisions will not be included in OAH decisions. In most cases, resolved in Alternative Dispute Resolution will also have some nondisclosure agreement to hide the school's behavior and conduct and protect the reputation of its staff, school board, or superintendent.

THE SECRET
AUTISM ROADMAP

Transitioning to Adulthood

"The personality – focused job application process is a barrier for many people who may be better at performing the job then at talking about themselves - and it is just one example of the many workplace "norms" that are not inclusive of neurodiversity."

— Harvard Business Review

THE SECRET

The secret is this has been the goal of advocating and providing therapy, services, and programs for your child since they were first diagnosed. Transitioning to adulthood is difficult for any young adult and doubly difficult for someone with autism. As programs are developed, carefully think of the end goals.

- **PLAN EARLY**
  The transition planning process should start as early as possible, preferably around the age of 14-16, during the IEP process.

- **CREATE A TRANSITION PLAN**
  A transition plan should address the individual's needs, preferences, and goals and should include post-secondary education, employment, independent living, and community engagement.

- **FOCUS ON INDEPENDENT LIVING SKILLS**
  Certain skills can be essential for individuals living independently or in supported living arrangements. These skills include managing finances, cooking, household chores, transportation, and personal care.

- **IDENTIFY COMMUNITY RESOURCES**
  Identify community resources and support services to help individuals achieve their goals. This may include vocational training programs, job coaches, and housing assistance.

- **DEVELOP SOCIAL SKILLS**
  Help the individual develop social skills to facilitate meaningful social interactions.

- **ENCOURAGE SELF-ADVOCACY**
  Encourage the individual to develop self-advocacy skills, which can help them communicate their needs and preferences effectively.

- **MONITOR PROGRESS**
  Regularly djust the transition plan to ensure the individual is on track to achieve their goals.

The Economics of Adults with Autism

The majority of autism's costs in the U.S. are for adult services – an estimated $200 billion a year for adults, compared to $66 billion a year for children.

$461
BILLION

The cost of caring for Americans
with Autism in 2025

$268
BILLION

The cost of caring for Americans
with Autism in 2015

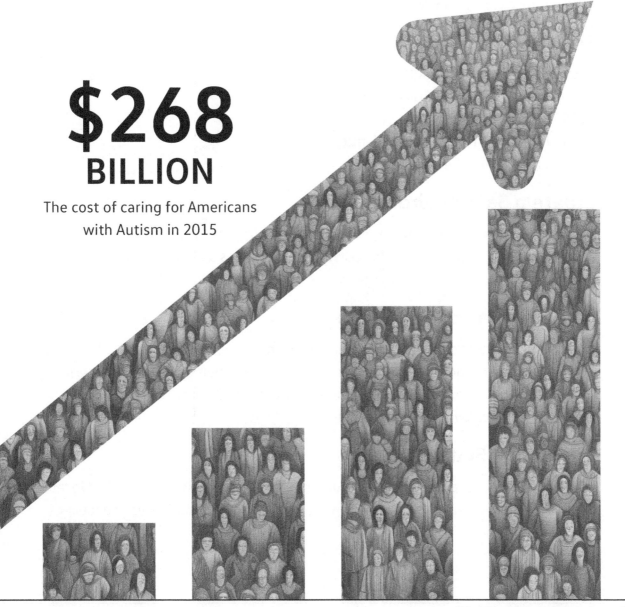

When to Discuss Autism

Discussing an autism diagnosis with a person is a sensitive and important matter that requires careful consideration. It is a gradual and ongoing process. It may take time to understand and integrate the information into their self-concept. Be patient, supportive, and responsive to the child's needs throughout this journey. There is no one-size-fits-all answer to this question, as the timing will depend on the child's age, level of understanding, and individual needs.

Age and Developmental Level

Young children may not have the cognitive capacity to comprehend the concept of autism fully. It is generally recommended to wait until a child is at least 7 years old.

Positive Framing

Emphasize the child's strengths and unique qualities while discussing the autism diagnosis. Help them understand that autism is just one aspect of their identity and does not define their identity.

Create a Safe Environment

Choose a quiet and comfortable space for the conversation where the child feels safe and supported. Be prepared to answer their questions and address any concerns they may have.

Be Patient and Supportive

Accept that the child's reaction to the diagnosis may vary. Some children might take the news in stride, and some may use it as an excuse for being unable to do certain things, while others might need more time to process and come to terms with it. Offer reassurance, love, and ongoing support.

Encourage Self-Advocacy

As the child ages, empower them to understand their diagnosis better and advocate for their needs. Encourage open communication about their experiences and feelings related to autism.

Proper Hygiene and Grooming

Addressing proper hygiene and grooming may require additional strategies and accommodations to meet their unique needs. Be gentle, supportive, and understanding, and work together to establish healthy hygiene and grooming habits that suit their individual needs.

Create a Hygiene Chart

Use visual schedules or step-by-step picture guides to help understand the hygiene routine. Visual cues can make the process more predictable and less overwhelming.

Modeling and Imitation

Kids learn by observing others. Demonstrate the proper hygiene and grooming practices yourself, and encourage the child to imitate your actions.

Break Tasks Down

If certain hygiene routines involve multiple steps, break them into smaller, manageable tasks. Focus on one step at a time and gradually build up to the full routine.

Use Preferred Products

Some children with autism may have sensory sensitivities. Allow them to choose grooming products they feel comfortable using, such as specific soaps, shampoos, or toothpaste.

Use Countdowns or Timers

Some children with autism may struggle with transitions. Give them a warning before starting grooming activities, and use timers to signal the end of the task.

Visual Prompts in the Bathroom

Place visual prompts or reminders in the bathroom to guide the child through washing hands, brushing teeth, etc.

College Accommodations

Colleges and universities typically have a department or office dedicated to supporting and accommodating students with disabilities, including autism. By working with them, your child's accommodations and supports from high-school can be carried over to college or university.

Accommodations and supports are not automatically transferred to your college or university, so it is imperative to start working with your college or universities Disability Services Office early. They serve as the primary point of contact for requesting accommodations and provide guidance on how their system works and how to ensure accommodations and support are in place. Some of the accommodations are:

- **EXTENDED TEST TIME**
  Allowing sufficient time to process questions and demonstrate their knowledge without feeling rushed.

- **NOTE-TAKING ASSISTANCE**
  Note-taking assistance includes a Note-taker who shares their notes to ensure they have complete and organized information.

- **PRIORITY REGISTRATION**
  Allows you to select their preferred class schedules and arrange for classes at times when they are best able to focus and function.

- **DISTRACTION-FREE TESTING**
  Minimizes sensory overload and distractions during exams.

- **ASSISTIVE TECHNOLOGY**
  Access to assistive technologies, such as speech-to-text software or other tools to aid with reading, writing, and communication.

SOCIAL SKILLS SUPPORT
  Social skills training or counseling to help navigate social situations and build relationships on campus.

- **FLEXIBILITY WITH ASSIGNMENTS**
  Flexibility with assignment due dates to accommodate the individual needs.

- **SENSORY SUPPORT**
  Sensory support rooms or spaces can be beneficial for taking breaks.

- **PEER MENTORING PROGRAMS**
  Peer mentoring programs can offer guidance, support, and practical tips for navigating college life.

- **ACCESSIBILITY ACCOMMODATIONS**
  Campuses are working to ensure accessibility across campus for students with disabilities, including making physical spaces, digital resources more accessible.

Department of Rehabilitation

The Department of Rehabilitation (DOR) is a government agency in the United States that provides vocational rehabilitation services to individuals with disabilities. Its primary mission is to assist people with disabilities in obtaining and maintaining meaningful employment or achieving greater independence in their daily lives. The specific services and programs offered by the Department of Rehabilitation can vary from state to state, as each state operates its own DOR under federal guidelines.

- **VOCATIONAL COUNSELING**
  DOR offers vocational counseling to help explore career options, identify their strengths and interests, and set vocational goals. In some states the DOR assists with college costs.

- **VOCATIONAL TRAINING**
  May provide job-related training or skills development programs to enhance a person's employability in specific industries or professions.

- **JOB PLACEMENT**
  DOR helps find suitable employment opportunities by connecting them with employers and facilitating job placements.

- **ASSISTIVE TECHNOLOGY**
  May offer access to assistive technologies and devices that help individuals with disabilities perform job-related tasks more effectively.

- **JOB COACHING AND SUPPORT**
  May provide job coaching services, where a professional assists the individual in learning job tasks and adjusting to the workplace.

- **TRANSITION SERVICES**
  Works with young adults transitioning from high school to post-secondary education or the workforce, providing guidance and support during this critical phase.

- **INDEPENDENT LIVING SERVICES**
  Offer programs and support to help live independently, including access to housing resources and daily living assistance.

- **REHABILITATION TECHNOLOGY SERVICES**
  Includes the evaluation and provision of assistive technology devices and services promoting independence and workforce integration.

- **ADVOCACY AND RIGHTS PROTECTION**
  The DOR may advocate for the rights to remove barriers to employment and equal opportunities.

Autism Employment Outlook

In the United States, autistic employees have faced an uphill battle to secure steady employment.

National Autistic Society

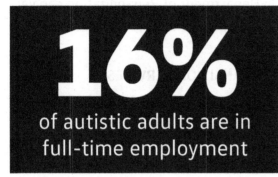

16% of autistic adults are in full-time employment

32% are in some kind of paid work

Office for National Statistics (ONS)

We are really worried that out of all disabled people, autistic people seem to have the worst employment rate.

While not all autistic people can work, we know most want to.

22% autistic people reported being in any paid work

Many challenges need to be overcome. The first step is identifying them.

- **EMPLOYMENT BARRIERS**
  There are significant barriers to employment, including prejudice, discrimination, and lack of understanding from employers.

- **INTERVIEW AND COMMUNICATION DIFFICULTIES:**
  Many people struggle with traditional interview formats and specific aspects of communication and social interaction required in the workplace.

- **SENSORY SENSITIVITIES**
  Some individuals have sensitivities that can be challenging in specific work environments, such as open layouts or strong smells or bright lights.

- **DIFFICULTY WITH SOCIAL CUES**
  Interpreting social cues is often tricky, affecting workplace dynamics.

How Challenges are Being Overcome

Developing processes to better integrate people on the spectrum into the workplace is vital for both social and economic reasons. It helps tap into the talents and capabilities of a diverse workforce, promotes equal opportunities, and contributes to a more inclusive society by raising awareness. Groups like Neurodiversity @ Work Employer Roundtable developed the Disability Equality Index (DEI) to help companies develop a disability-inclusive landscape. The DEI incorporates practices that facilitate inclusive workplaces and set goals driven by inclusive values, which are:

- **UNIQUE SKILLS AND STRENGTHS**
  Many autistic individuals possess unique talents and strengths, such as attention to detail, pattern recognition, and strong analytical abilities. These qualities can be valuable in work settings, including technology, research, and creative fields.

- **DIVERSE PERSPECTIVES:**
  Embracing neurodiversity in the workforce brings diverse perspectives and approaches to problem-solving, fostering innovation and creativity.

- **WORKPLACE ACCOMMODATIONS**
  With appropriate accommodations and support, autistic individuals can thrive in the workplace. Simple adjustments, such as flexible work arrangements or clear communication guidelines, can contribute to their success.

Workplace Accommodations

By creating a supportive and inclusive work environment, employers can help foster the success and well-being of autistic individuals in the workforce. Various accommodations can be made to support autistic individuals. These accommodations aim to create an environment that enables autistic employees to thrive and perform to the best of their abilities.

SENSORY CONSIDERATIONS:

- Providing a quiet or low-stimulus workspace or a sensory-friendly area.

- Allowing the use of noise-canceling headphones or providing white noise machines.

- Adjusting lighting levels or providing access to natural light.

- Allowing breaks or flexible work schedules to help with sensory overload.

COMMUNICATION AND SOCIAL INTERACTIONS:

- Provide clear instructions or written communication when assigning tasks.

- Offering visual aids, such as visible schedules or checklists, to help with task organization and planning.

- Implementing communication preferences, such as email or instant messaging, for individuals struggling with verbal communication.

- Provide social skills training or coaching to help navigate social interactions in the workplace.

WORK ENVIRONMENT AND ROUTINE:

- Allowing for a consistent routine or schedule to provide predictability and reduce anxiety.

- Offering flexibility in work hours or location, including remote work options.

- Providing structured and well-defined job roles and responsibilities.

- Offering support in transitions between tasks in the work environment.

SUPPORT AND RESOURCES:

- Assign a mentor or buddy to provide guidance and support.

- Offer additional training or professional development opportunities.

- Provide access to assistive technologies or software that can enhance productivity with specific challenges.

- Establishing employee resource groups or affinity groups focused on neurodiversity for support.

Assistance with Employment

Interviewing for a job is very difficult, but assistance and supports are available. Here are some resources and strategies that can be helpful:

- **VOCATIONAL REHABILITATION SERVICES**
  Vocational rehabilitation agencies offer job training, career counseling, and assistance with job placement.

- **AUTISM-SPECIFIC ORGANIZATIONS**
  Numerous organizations like Autism Speaks, Autism Society, Autism Employment Network, Asperger's/Autism Network (AANE), Job Accommodation Network (JAN), and Autism Works specialize in supporting individuals with Autism in various aspects of life, including employment. They offer resources, workshops, and programs tailored to help navigate the job application process.

- **JOB COACHES AND EMPLOYMENT SUPPORT SPECIALISTS**
  Job coaches or employment support specialists can work one-on-one to provide personalized guidance throughout the job application process. They can help with resume writing, interview preparation, and job search strategies.

- **AUTISM-FRIENDLY EMPLOYERS**
  Employers like Microsoft, SAP, Hewlett Packard, JPMorgan Chase, Ford Motor Company, Ernst & Young, and Walgreens have demonstrated a commitment to promoting inclusivity in the workplace.

- **NETWORKING AND MENTORSHIP**
  Building a professional network and seeking mentorship from individuals already employed in your desired field can be beneficial. Attend job fairs, industry events, or join professional organizations to connect with people who can offer guidance and potential job opportunities.

- **ONLINE JOB SEARCH PLATFORMS**
  Utilize special needs online job search platforms like Specialisterne, Getting Hired, Neurodiversity in the Workplace, AbilityJobs, and Neurodiversity Job Boards. These platforms can help you identify job opportunities with companies that value diversity and inclusion.

- **GOVERNMENT PROGRAMS AND INCENTIVES**
  In the United States, incentives like Work Opportunity Tax Credit (WOTC) and Disability Employment Initiative (DEI) encourage employers to hire individuals with disabilities. These initiatives can include tax credits, wage subsidies, and other forms of support for the employee and the employer.

Masking

People in the workforce often hide or suppress their autistic traits and behaviors to fit social expectations and norms. This is called masking. Masking can help individuals navigate social situations more smoothly by aligning their behavior with societal norms and expectations. This can enhance their chances of acceptance and inclusion in social interactions and avoid stigmatization or negative stereotypes associated with autism.

Masking isn't universal. It tends to be more prevalent among individuals who have learned to camouflage their autistic traits in order to navigate social situations more easily. However, masking can come at a cost, as it requires individuals to constantly monitor and modify their behavior to fit social expectations, which can be mentally and emotionally draining. The effort involved in masking can lead to increased stress, anxiety, and a sense of exhaustion over time.

Supportive environments, understanding friends and family, and access to appropriate accommodations and therapies can help individuals with autism manage masking exhaustion and find a balance between fitting into social expectations and maintaining their well-being.

Dating

Dating can present particular challenges for autistic individuals, but it's important to remember that experiences and difficulties vary widely. Here are some common challenges that autistic individuals may encounter when it comes to dating:

COMMUNICATION DIFFERENCES

There can be struggles with social cues and nonverbal communication. There are also unwritten rules of dating that can lead to confusion, frustration, or unintended miscommunication.

SENSORY SENSITIVITIES

Loud or crowded environments, bright lights, strong smells, or physical touch may be overwhelming or uncomfortable, making it hard to enjoy dating activities.

DIFFICULTY EXPRESSING EMOTIONS

Identifying feelings, as well as understanding other's emotions.

MANAGING ANXIETY

Dating scenarios may involve crowded or noisy places, unfamiliar people, or high-pressure situations. This can increase anxiety levels, making it more challenging for autistic individuals to relax and enjoy the experience.

CHALLENGES WITH FLEXIBILITY

The unpredictable nature of dating, including unexpected plans, changes in routine or adapting to new social situations can be stressful or anxiety provoking.

DATING IN THE DIGITAL AGE

Social media offers ways for people with specific interests to meet and discuss issues of interest. Numerous websites are designed to support those on the autism spectrum that want to pursue relationships or friendships and better themselves.

A few of these websites are:

AUTISTIC DATING www. autistic-dating.com

ASPIE SINGLES www.aspie-singles.com

HIKI www.hikiapp.com

MEET UP www.meetup.com

UNEEPI www.uneepi.com

Housing

Various housing options are available for adults with autism, depending on their individual needs, preferences, and level of independence. It is crucial to consider the specific needs and preferences of the individual with autism when exploring housing options. It's advisable to consult with local disability service providers, social workers, and housing agencies to identify options and determine the best fit for each individual's circumstances. Here are some standard housing options:

- **INDEPENDENT LIVING**
  This option allows them to develop essential life skills while maintaining control over their living environment.

- **SUPPORTED LIVING PROGRAMS**
  Supported living programs provide the opportunity to live in a semi-independent setting with varying levels of support. These programs offer assistance with daily living tasks, socialization, and community integration while promoting independence.

- **GROUP HOMES**
  Group homes, or residential care facilities, are shared living environments where individuals with autism live with support staff who provide assistance.

- **TRANSITIONAL HOUSING**
  Transitional housing programs are designed to support individuals transitioning from dependence to independence. These programs provide a structured and supportive living environment while offering opportunities for skill development and self-sufficiency.

- **COMMUNITY-BASED HOUSING**
  Community-based housing refers to integrating into regular residential neighborhoods. This can include living in apartments, condominiums, or houses with the necessary services and accommodations.

- **CO-HOUSING**
  Co-housing is an arrangement where individuals live in a cooperative community, sharing common spaces and resources while maintaining their living units. Co-housing emphasize mutual support, responsibilities, and social interaction.

- **FAMILY-BASED ARRANGEMENTS**
  Some adults with autism may choose to live with family members in the family home or an accessory dwelling unit. This arrangement can provide a familiar and supportive environment.

Housing Assistance

It's recommended to contact these organizations, explore their websites, and contact them directly for more information and specific assistance tailored to the individual's location and housing needs. Local disability service providers, social workers, and housing agencies can provide valuable guidance and support in accessing housing resources. While the availability of housing assistance may vary depending on the location, here are some organizations that offer support and resources related to housing:

- **AUTISM HOUSING NETWORK** www.autismhousingnetwork.org
  The Autism Housing Network is an online platform that offers information, resources and a searchable directory of housing options for individuals with autism. They guide various housing models, including community-based alternatives, and offer tools to navigate the housing process.

- **AUTISM SPEAKS** www.autismspeaks.org
  Autism Speaks is a well-known autism advocacy organization that provides resources and information on various aspects of autism, including housing.

- **THE ARC** www.thearc.org
  The Arc is a national organization that advocates for individuals with intellectual and developmental disabilities. They also offer local chapters resources and support related to housing options, community living, and advocacy.

- **LOCAL HOUSING AUTHORITIES**
  Local housing authorities may provide housing assistance and resources.

- **STATE DEVELOPMENTAL DISABILITIES AGENCIES**
  State developmental disabilities agencies often have resources and programs related to housing. They can provide information on supportive housing options, funding sources, and housing-related assistance programs available within the state.

- **HOUSING AND URBAN DEVELOPMENT (HUD)** www.hud.gov
  HUD offers various housing assistance programs and resources, such as Section 8 vouchers and supportive housing programs that apply to individuals with disabilities.

THE SECRET
AUTISM ROADMAP

Parent
and Sibling
Self Care

"Keep Calm and Take a Sensory Break."
— *Unknow Author*

THE SECRET

Your mental health is the most important thing. Caregiving for an autistic child can be demanding and challenging, both physically and emotionally. Daily responsibilities, such as managing therapy appointments, advocating for the child's needs, and addressing behavioral challenges, can lead to high levels of stress, exhaustion, and burnout. Focusing on your mental health and well-being helps to build resilience, cope with stress, and prevent burnout, enabling you to provide consistent and effective care for your child.

Caring for an autistic child can be overwhelming and emotionally taxing. You need good mental health helps to approach these tasks with clarity and focus, and effectively accessing the necessary resources. It also empowers them to be strong advocates for their child's needs, ensuring they receive appropriate support and services.

Finally, a caregiver's mental well-being directly impacts the overall family dynamics and the child's environment. When caregivers prioritize their mental health, they can create a positive and supportive home environment for their autistic child. This environment promotes emotional stability, understanding, and patience, essential for the child's development and well-being.

Prioritizing mental health isn't easy for someone caring for an autistic child. Still, it is vital to preventing caregiver burnout, enhancing resilience, navigating support systems effectively, and creating a positive home environment.

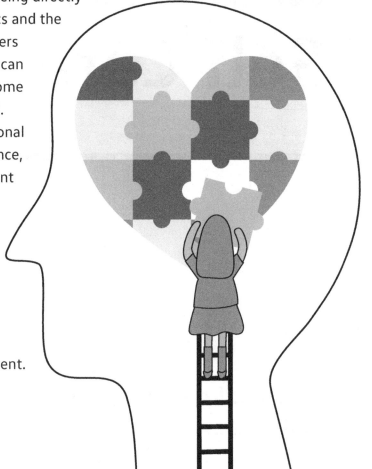

Feeling Like You Failed Your Child

It is very common for a parent of an autistic child to feel like they have failed their child. They miss the life they had before they had a child with special needs. It is very understandable to feel this way. Many parents struggle to get services for their child, and when they do get a service or program in place, it shows itself to be ineffective or only provide minimal gains. Sometimes it is difficult to evaluate progress over a long period of time, and sometime it is good time to reevaluate your current program or lack of program.

VALIDATE YOUR FEELINGS

Sometimes it is normal to feel overwhelmed, frustrated, or even a sense of failure. It is common for parents of autistic child to struggle.

LOOK FOR INFORMATION AND RESOURCES

Look for resources such as books, websites, support groups, and professional contacts that can offer guidance and support.

ENCOURAGE SELF-CARE

Prioritize your physical and emotional well-being by engaging in activities they enjoy

EVALUATE YOUR CURRENT THERAPY PROGRAM

Is your current therapy program not addressing problematic behaviors or providing the training you need? Document your problem issues and put a new program in place.

FIND YOUR CHILD'S STRENGTHS

The National Autism Association is a non-profit organization that provides support and advocacy for families affected by autism.

BUILD A SOCIAL NETWORK

Connect with support networks and communities that can provide understanding and guidance.

Support Groups

Finding a support group that fits your or your loved one's specific needs and interests is crucial. A support group helps reduce feelings of isolation and promotes social interaction and support. Additionally, support groups offer a platform for sharing knowledge, strategies, and resources, enabling members to learn from each other's experiences and gain valuable insights into autism-related issues. These groups also provide emotional support and validation, allowing individuals to express their concerns, fears, and triumphs in a safe and non-judgmental environment

AUTISM SPEAK
Autism Speaks is a national advocacy organization that provides resources, support, and education for individuals with autism and their families.

AUTISM SOCIETY
The Autism Society is a national advocacy organization that provides information, resources, and support for individuals with autism and their families.

NATIONAL AUTISM ASSOCIATION
The National Autism Association is a non-profit organization that provides support and advocacy for families affected by autism.

ASPERGER'S/AUTISM NETWORK
The Asperger's/Autism Network is a non-profit organization that provides support, education, and resources for individuals with Asperger's syndrome and autism.

ONLINE SUPPORT GROUPS
Many online support groups, forums, and blogs are available online, as well as groups on Tik Tok, Facebook, and Instagram. These groups allow individuals to connect with others who share similar experiences and offer a sense of community and support.

LOCAL SUPPORT GROUPS
Local support groups or SELPAs in your area may provide in-person support and resources for individuals with autism and their families. These groups provide a valuable opportunity for individuals to connect with others and access local resources and services.

Tips for Mental Health

Prioritizing mental health is an ongoing process, and finding strategies that work best for you is important. Try a few of these tips and gradually build on them.

- Practice self-care regularly, even in small ways.
- Set boundaries and communicate your needs to others.
- Seek support from other caregivers who understand your experiences.
- Take breaks and permit yourself to rest.
- Prioritize quality sleep and establish a bedtime routine.
- Engage in physical exercise or activities that you enjoy.
- Practice deep breathing or mindfulness techniques to manage stress.
- Engage in hobbies or activities that bring you joy and relaxation.
- Practice gratitude and focus on positive aspects of your life.
- Create a routine or schedule that includes time for self-care.
- Delegate tasks and ask for help.
- Practice time management and prioritize tasks.
- Maintain a balanced and nutritious diet.
- Limit exposure to negative news or social media.

- Engage in activities that promote laughter and humor.
- Seek professional therapy or counseling if needed.
- Practice effective communication and assertiveness skills.
- Engage in activities that promote creativity and self-expression.
- Engage in activities that promote social connection.
- Take time for yourself each day, even just a few minutes.
- Practice relaxation techniques such as meditation or yoga.
- Engage in activities that promote personal growth and learning.
- Create a calming and organized environment at home.
- Find outlets for emotional expressions, such as journaling, gardening, or art.
- Engage in activities promoting sensory relaxation, such as bathing or listening to calming music.
- Foster a support network of friends, family, or support groups.
- Celebrate small victories and acknowledge your efforts.

Siblings and an Autistic Child

Having an autistic sibling is similar to having typically developing siblings – enriching and challenging. For example, siblings of children with disability, including autistic children, are often exceptionally caring, compassionate, independent, tolerant, and responsive to the needs of others.

EMBARRASSMENT

Children are judgmental people. And, unlike adults, they can pass judgment out loud in public. No neurotypically developing child finds it easy or pleasant to hear their peers ask, "What's wrong with your sibling?

RESENTMENT

When a sibling has autism, the entire family must adjust. It is essential to tend to typical siblings to prevent resentment towards their autistic loved ones.

EXPECTATIONS

When there is a disabled family member, other family members must help support them, including siblings.

FINANCES

If money is going to provide services for the autistic child, little may be left for other children. College funds may go toward autism therapy, while second mortgages may pay for fitting schools for autistic children or respite care.

FAMILY ATTITUDES

Autism aside, family attitudes and situations can significantly impact children. Add autism into the mix, and ordinary family conflicts, challenges, strengths, and flexibility become huge.

HELP DEVELOPING CHILD

Whatever your circumstances and the abilities and challenges of your autistic child, it's essential to keep your neurotypically developing child's needs in mind.

Sibling Relationships

Building a healthy sibling relationship takes time and effort. Having a sibling with autism can be difficult. The sibling might get thrown in as a caretaker with little understanding of autism. This can build resentment, so it is essential to maintain open lines of communication, address any issues or concerns promptly, and ensure that both siblings feel valued, supported, and loved. Each family's dynamics and circumstances may vary, so tailor these strategies to fit your specific situation and the unique needs of your children.

EDUCATION AND AWARENESS

Providing age-appropriate information about autism to the sibling to can help them understand their sibling's unique challenges and differences. Encourage open conversations about autism, addressing questions and concerns the sibling may have.

INDIVIDUAL ATTENTION AND QUALITY TIME

Ensure the sibling without autism receives individual attention and quality time with parents or caregivers. Plan activities that they enjoy and create opportunities for meaningful interactions.

SUPPORTIVE SIBLING RELATIONSHIPS

Encourage positive interactions and shared experiences between siblings. Facilitate activities that allow them to bond and build a strong sibling relationships. Celebrate accomplishments and milestones together, fostering a sense of unity and connection.

Sibling Involvement and Empowerment

Involve the sibling in their autistic sibling's care and therapy when appropriate. Encourage them to participate in activities that promote their involvement and understanding. Empowering the sibling with knowledge and skills can enhance their sense of contribution and participation in their sibling's journey.

Keeping Things Fun

Families can engage in various activities that are inclusive and enjoyable for both children and a child with autism. Here are some ideas:

SENSORY-FRIENDLY OUTINGS

Plan outings to places that offer sensory-friendly experiences, such as sensory-friendly events or walks.

FAMILY GAME NIGHTS

Engage in board, card, or interactive video games that the whole family can enjoy.

CRAFTS AND COOKING

Explore artistic activities like drawing, painting, or sculpting. Involve your children in preparing meals or baking treats together.

OUTDOOR ACTIVITIES

Enjoy outdoor adventures as a family, such as hiking, picnicking, or visiting a local park.

MAKE NEW TRADITIONS

Reevalute traditions. Why shouldn't a Thanksgiving dinner include a pizza or special characters be included in Christmas decorations?

STORYTIME AND READING

Read stories together as a family. Choose books that align with your childen's interests and abilities.

ANIMAL INTERACTIONS

Visit petting zoos or aquariums where your children can safely interact with animals.

RELAXATION ACTIVITIES

Mindfulness activities as a family, such as yoga, deep breathing exercises, or guided meditation.

Tips for Taking a Trip

Going on a vacation or taking a trip to visit relatives can be very challenging in the best of situations, but taking a child that has trouble with changes in routine or unfamiliar setting is extremely difficult.

Plan and prepare in advance. Use social stories, videos, and visual schedules. Then, be ready to adjust the trip as needed for a positive experience.

- **PLAN AHEAD**

  Plan the trip and involve the child. Practice going over what will happen on the trip and how they should behave. This can help reduce anxiety and uncertainty.

- **STICK TO A ROUTINE**

  Maintaining a consistent routine as much as possible. Use a visual schedule to help the child mentally prepare for the day and events.

- **FAMILIARIZE WITH THE DESTINATION**

  Show the child pictures and videos of the destination, and discuss what will happen and what to expect.

- **PACK FAMILIAR ITEMS**

  Take familiar items such as toys, and clothing to provide comfort and familiarity.

- **ALLOW FOR DOWNTIME**

  Plan for quiet and relaxing activities and allow ample downtime to recharge.

- **BE PATIENT AND UNDERSTANDING**

  Travel can be stressful for anyone. Be patient, understanding, and flexible. Remember, family members might make comments or give you parenting suggestions. Usually, they have little knowledge of Autism and do not understand therapy techniques or sensory issues.

- **LOOK FOR SPECIALISTS**

  Often, events or excursions have people familiar with special needs who can lead your group and provide special assistance as needed.

Dealing with Difficult Grandparents or Family Members

Dealing with grandparents who don't accept an autistic grandchild or criticize parenting styles can be challenging. Numerous complaints exist about how people have estranged themselves from grandparents or family members. Your child's grandparents may have never met a child with autism. Try to promote understanding, open communication, and a supportive environment for your child. Here are some suggestions for handling this situation:

EDUCATE & SHARE INFORMATION

Provide your grandparents with accurate information about autism. Help them understand it is neurological, not parenting.

OPEN DIALOGUE

Initiate a respectful and open conversation with your grandparents. Express your concerns about their lack of acceptance or critical comments.

SHARE PERSONAL EXPERIENCES

Share your experiences as a parent. Help your grandparents understand the joys, and challenges.

SET BOUNDARIES

If your grandparents continue to make derogatory comments or refuse to accept your child, and it may be necessary to establish clear boundaries.

SEEK PROFESSIONAL GUIDANCE

If the situation persists or becomes more challenging, consider involving a professional, such as a family therapist or counselor.

FIND SUPPORT NETWORKS

These communities can provide a safe space to share experiences, receive advice, and seek emotional support.

Respite Care

Respite care is a temporary break or relief for individuals who care for someone with a disability or chronic condition, including autism. The purpose of respite care is to give the caregiver a break from their caregiving responsibilities and allow them to recharge and renew their energy.

Researching the different options and finding a respite care provider that meets your needs is essential. To learn more about respite care options in your area, you can contact local organizations serving individuals with autism, such as the Autism Society or your state's Department of Developmental Services.

There are several ways to obtain respite care, including:

IN-HOME RESPITE

This type of respite care provides temporary care in the individual's home, allowing the caregiver to take a break from their responsibilities.

RESPITE PROGRAMS

Many organizations and service providers offer respite care programs that provide temporary care in a safe and supportive environment.

RESPITE VOUCHERS

Some state and federal programs offer respite vouchers, which can be used to pay for in-home respite or respite programs.

RESPITE PROVIDERS

There are private respite providers that offer care, either in the individual's home or in a respite care facility.

SSI — Supplemental Security Income

SSI, or Supplemental Security Income, is a federal program that provides financial assistance to individuals with disabilities, including autism. The program is administered by the Social Security Administration (SSA) and is based on financial need. To qualify for SSI, an individual must have limited income and assets and meet the SSA's definition of disability, which includes having a condition that significantly limits their ability to perform basic activities of daily living such as communication, social interaction, and learning.

For individuals with autism, a diagnosis of the condition alone does not guarantee eligibility for SSI benefits. WHEN DETERMINING ELIGIBILITY, the SSA will consider the individual's specific limitations, such as difficulty with communication and social interaction. The SSA may also require additional medical evidence, such as reports from doctors or therapists, to determine the extent of the individual's limitations and eligibility.

The SSI Application Process

It is important to note that the application process for a Supplemental Security Income (SSI) may vary depending on your location. It is recommended to consult with the Social Security Administration or seek assistance from a disability advocate or attorney who specializes in SSI applications to ensure you have accurate and up-to-date information specific to your situation.

Here are the general steps:

1 GATHER NECESSARY INFORMATION

Collect important documents and any documentation related to the diagnosis.

2 DETERMINE ELIGIBILITY

Review the eligibility criteria for SSI to ensure the individual meets the requirements, including income and resource limits. SSI is a needs-based program, so financial eligibility is a key factor.

3 CONTACT THE SOCIAL SECURITY ADMINISTRATION (SSA)

Reach out to the SSA to begin the application process. You can contact them by calling their toll-free number at 1-800-772-1213 or visiting a local SSA office.

4 COMPLETE THE APPLICATION

Fill out the SSI application form. Provide accurate and detailed information about the individual's condition, functional limitations, and financial situation.

5 MEDICAL EVALUATION

The SSA may require a medical evaluation to assess the individual's disability. They may ask for additional records or schedule a consultative examination.

6 FINANCIAL EVALUATION

SSA will evaluate the individual's income and resources to determine eligibility.

7 AWAIT A DECISION

After submitting the application, you will receive a decision from the SSA regarding eligibility for SSI. This can take months, so be prepared to wait.

8 APPEAL IF NECESSARY

Is is quite common for the first application to be denied, but you have the right to appeal the decision. Follow the instructions provided by the SSA to initiate an appeal and provide any additional information or documentation.

IHH — Medicaid Home and Community-Based Services (HCBS)

IHH refers to the Medicaid Home and Community-Based Services (HCBS), which may provide financing for certain services and supports that enable a spouse or a family member to care for a child with autism at home. The program is intended to provide individuals with autism with support to live in the community rather than in institutions.

To be eligible for the IHH waiver program, individuals with autism must meet Medicaid financial eligibility requirements and be diagnosed with an Intellectual and Developmental Disability. In addition, the individual must require a level of care that would otherwise be provided in a hospital or nursing facility. The IHH waiver program offers a range of services to eligible individuals, including assistance with daily living activities, support in the community, and access to medical and behavioral health services.

The program is designed to be flexible, allowing individuals to receive services in their homes and communities rather than in institutions. The specific services provided under the IHH waiver program can vary by state and individual, depending on their needs and goals. However, the program is intended to help individuals with autism to live as independently as possible while still receiving the support they need to be safe and successful in their communities.

The IHH Application Process

The Medicaid Home and Community-Based Services (HCBS) application process varies depending on your location and the specific program available in your area. It is recommended to contact your local Medicaid office or seek assistance from a Medicaid enrollment counselor or advocate who can provide guidance.

Here are the general steps:

1 DETERMINE ELIGIBILITY

Review the eligibility criteria for Medicaid HCBS in your state. Eligibility requirements may vary, but generally, individuals with who require long-term support and meet functional and financial criteria may qualify for HCBS.

2 GATHER NECESSARY INFORMATION

Collect important documents such as identification documents, Social Security numbers, proof of income, medical records, and any documentation related to the individual's diagnosis and need for home and community-based services.

3 CONTACT THE MEDICAID OFFICE

Local Medicaid office or the designated agency responsible for administering HCBS programs can provide guidance on the application process.

4 COMPLETE THE APPLICATION

Fill out the Medicaid HCBS application form. Provide accurate information about the individual's medical condition, functional limitations, and need for home and community-based services.

5 FINANCIAL EVALUATION

Medicaid will evaluate the individual's income and resources to determine financial eligibility.

6 FUNCTIONAL ASSESSMENT

The Medicaid agency may conduct a functional assessment. This assessment helps determine the level of support and specific services required.

7 AWAIT A DECISION

After submitting the application the timeframe for processing applications can vary, so be prepared for some waiting time

8 APPEAL IF NECESSARY

It isn't surprising applications for applications to be denied on the first attempt. Follow the instructions provided by Medicaid to initiate an appeal and provide any additional information or documentation needed.

Marriage Pressures

Divorce rates among parents of a child with autism are higher than the general population, with some studies reporting rates as high as 85%. It is important to note that divorce is not inevitable for parents of a child with autism. Many families can successfully navigate the challenges of caring for a child with autism while maintaining a strong and healthy relationship. By seeking support, caring for their mental health, and finding ways to manage stress and conflict, parents can improve their chances of avoiding divorce and building a happy and healthy family. This is thought to be due to several factors, including:

INCREASED STRESS

Caring for a child with autism can be challenging and can place significant demands on the relationship. The stress of dealing with therapy, and behavior issues can take a toll on the relationship and lead to conflict.

FINANCIAL STRAIN

Autism can be expensive, and many families struggle to meet the costs of therapy, special equipment, and other related expenses. Financial stress can further increase the tension in the relationship.

REDUCED QUALITY TIME

The demands of caring for a child with autism can reduce the time and energy that parents have for each other, leading to a breakdown in communication and intimacy.

LACK OF SUPPORT

Many parents of children with autism feel isolated and struggle to find support. This can increase stress, resentment, and desperation, further damaging the relationship.

Tips for a Successful Marriage

Marriage is tough, and having a child with special needs can bring additional stress and challenges. Here are some tips for parents to try and work together to maintain a strong relationship.

COMMUNICATE OPENLY

Regularly discuss your feelings, expectations, and challenges related to your child's autism and how you can support each other.

SEEK SUPPORT

Consider seeking help from therapy, support groups, or counseling to address any conflicts and stress related to your child's autism.

DIVIDE AND CONQUER

Assign tasks and responsibilities according to each person's strengths and preferences.

PRIORITIZE SELF-CARE

Take care of your physical and emotional health, and encourage each other to do the same.

MAKE TIME

Set aside time for just the two of you to connect and have fun, even if it's just a few minutes a day.

FOCUS ON TEAMWORK

Work together as a team to provide the best support. Make sure not all the responsibility is put on one person.

THE SECRET AUTISM ROADMAP

Glossary

"In the special needs system, the paperwork and bureaucracy can often overshadow the needs of the individuals we're trying to help."

— Author Unknown

Special Education Glossary

ACCOMMODATIONS
Changes in an instructional or testing environment allow a student to access the curriculum and demonstrate their knowledge and skills. Accommodations can be grouped into thefollowing categories:

Accessible Educational Materials (AEM)
Textbooks and instructional materials that have been converted into a format that is accessible to a student who is unable to use standard printed materials.

Adapted Physical Education (APE)
The IEP team will recommend APE if your child cannot safely or successfully participate in the regular physical education program.

Alternate Assessment
Used to evaluate the performance and progress of students with severe cognitive disabilities who are unable to take part in standard assessments, even with testing accommodations.

ALTERNATE PLACEMENT
Temporary service is provided when a student's special class is not available.

ANNUAL GOALS
Specific, measurable goals written on the IEP describe what the student is expected to achieve in the disability-related area(s) over one year.

ANNUAL REVIEW
A meeting is held once a year to evaluate the student's progress, revise their IEP as needed, and determine their continued eligibility for special education services.

ANTECEDENT
The events that triggered or occurred before a behavior.

APPLIED BEHAVIOR ANALYSIS (ABA)
A type of behavioral therapy that uses a systematic and data-driven approach to change behavior.

ASSISTIVE TECHNOLOGY (AT)
An Assistive Technology Device is any piece of equipment, product, or system that is used to increase, maintain or improve the functional capabilities of a child with a disability.

AUDIOLOGICAL ASSESSMENT
A specialized hearing assessment is conducted to determine whether or not a student has a significant hearing loss/impairment.

AUTISM SPECTRUM DISORDER (ASD)
A neurodevelopmental disorder characterized by difficulties with social interaction, communication, and repetitive behaviors.

BEHAVIOR
An observable and measurable action performed by an individual.

BEHAVIORAL INTERVENTION PLAN (BIP)
A plan that is based on the results of a Functional Behavioral Assessment (FBA) to address problem behavior.

BEHAVIORAL THERAPY
A type of therapy that aims to teach new behaviors and improve social skills through positive reinforcement and other techniques.

BILINGUAL ASSESSMENT
An evaluation is conducted in both English and a child's home or native language.

CHAINING
The process of breaking down a complex behavior into smaller, simpler components and teaching each component individually.

CLASSROOM OBSERVATION

An observation of a student in their primary educational setting to see how the student learns and what behaviors they exhibit.

COGNITIVE BEHAVIORAL THERAPY (CBT)

A type of therapy that focuses on changing negative thought patterns and behaviors.

CONSEQUENCE

The events or stimuli that follow a behavior.

COMPLEMENTARY AND ALTERNATIVE THERAPIES

These may include interventions such as acupuncture, massage, and music therapy.

CONFIDENTIALITY

The DOE is to maintain the student's special education records ina manner that ensures that only appropriate staff has access.

DECLASSIFICATION SUPPORT SERVICES

Students who no longer need special education services are declassified after a reevaluation.

DIPLOMA OF ATTENDENCE

The local diploma is a high school diploma option available to students who have not met the requirements for a diploma.

DISCRETE TRIAL TRAINING (DTT)

A teaching method used in ABA that involves breaking down a skill into small steps and teaching each step individually using a structured, systematic approach.

DISABILITY CLASSIFICATION

Disability Classification refers to the type of disability that most affect a student's educational performance.

DUE PROCESS

Procedures that, by law, are used to ensure your child's rights to a Free Appropriate Public Education (FAPE) and your rights to be involved and have a complete understanding of that process.

DUE PROCESS COMPLAINT

Also called a Request for an Impartial Hearing, this is a written complaint filed by a parent or a school district involving any matter relating to the identification, evaluation, educational placement, or provision of a Free Appropriate Public Education to a student with a disability.

DUE PROCESS HEARING (IMPARTIAL HEARING)

A legal proceeding before an Impartial Hearing Officer who is not an employee of the DOE. The parents and the school district present arguments, witnesses, and evidence.

EARLY INTERVENTION

Supports families with children ages birth to 3 who have disabilities or developmental delays.

EVALUATION

The process of collecting information about a student's strengths and weaknesses to improve his or her educational program. The data collected through assessments, observations, and interviews will assist the team in determining the child's present levels of functioning and educational needs.

EXECUTIVE FUNCTIONING

The mental skills used to plan, prioritize, and carry out tasks.

EXTENDED SCHOOL YEAR SERVICES (ESY)

Extended school year services are special education programs and services provided during July and August. They may be recommended for students with disabilities who require special education over the summer to prevent substantial regression.

FREE APPROPRIATE PUBLIC EDUCATION (FAPE)

Special education programs and related services are provided at public expense, under public supervision and direction, and without charge to the parent.

FUNCTIONAL BEHAVIORAL ASSESSMENT (FBA)

A Functional Behavioral Assessment may be conducted to find the reasons for a behavior that may interfere with a student's ability to access education and will include possible interventions to address it.

GENERAL EDUCATION CURRICULUM

The body of knowledge and range of skills that all students, including students with disabilities, are expected to master.

GENERALIZATION

The transfer of learned behaviors to new situations and environments.

GOALS

Specific, measurable outcomes the student is expected to achieve through their education plan.

HIGH-FUNCTIONING AUTISM

A term used to describe individuals with autism who have higher cognitive and language abilities, but still struggle with social interaction.

HOME INSTRUCTION

Home instruction is an educational service that is provided to students with disabilities who are unable to attend school due to a medical or psychological condition.

INDEPENDENT ASSESSMENT

A parent may request an independent assessment at DOE expense if they disagrees with an assessment conducted by the School District.

INDIVIDUALIZED EDUCATION PLAN (IEP)

A written plan that outlines the educational goals, services, and supports for a student with a disability.

INDIVIDUALIZED EDUCATION PLAN (IEP) TEAM

The IEP team is a group of members who share information and work together to determine whether your child has a disability and requires special education services.

INDIVIDUALS WITH DISABILITIES EDUCATION ACT (IDEA)

The IDEA is a Federal law that gives students with disabilities the right to receive a Free Appropriate Public Education (FAPE) in the least restrictive environment.

INITIAL REFERRAL

The initial referral is a request that begins the special education evaluation process to determine whether the student has a disability and requires special education services.

INTERPRETER/TRANSLATOR

A person who speaks the parent's preferred language/mode of communication or the child's language and interprets meetings for the parent and assessments for the student.

LEAST RESTRICTIVE ENVIRONMENT (LRE)

The educational setting where a student can receive their special education services while also having the opportunity to interact with peers to the greatest extent appropriate.

LOW-FUNCTIONING AUTISM

A term used to describe individuals with autism who have lower cognitive and language abilities.

MEDIATION

Mediation is a confidential process allowing parties to resolve disputes without a formal due process hearing.

MODIFICATIONS

Changes to the instructional material or expectations that make it easier for a student to learn and participate.

NEGATIVE REINFORCEMENT

Reinforcement involves punishment or removing an aversive stimulus to increase the frequency of a behavior.

NEURODIVERGENT

A term used to describe individuals whose neurological development and functioning are atypical.

NEUROLOGICAL ASSESSMENT

A neurological assessment is conducted when a suspected neurological disorder that present through problems in daily functioning.

OBJECTIVES

Smaller, measurable steps that help the student progress towards their goals.

OCCUPATIONAL THERAPY (OT)

Occupational Therapy is a related service designed to help a child maintain, improve, or restore adaptive and functional skills.

ORIENTATION AND MOBILITY SERVICES

Services are designed to improve a child's use of spatial and environmental concepts.

PARAPROFESSIONAL (1-on-1)

An aide who assists students, an entire class, or an individual student.

PARENTAL CONSENT

Written agreement from the student's parent or guardian to allow the school to provide special education and related services.

PARENT MEMBER

A parent member is a parent of a child with a disability in the school district who participates in IEP meetings and assists a parent of a child with a known or suspected disability in making educational decisions for their child.

PLACEMENT

The educational setting where the student will receive their special education services.

POSITIVE REINFORCEMENT

Reinforcement with a desirable consequence to increase the frequency of a behavior.

PENDENCY

When a parent or the DOE requests an Impartial Hearing, the child must remain in their "last agreed upon placement" until the Impartial Hearing Process (including all appeals) is complete.

PRIOR WRITTEN NOTICE

This is a notification sent by the DOE to the parents(s). This notification will inform the parent(s) that the DOE is proposing to initiate or change the identification, and educational placement of their child.

PROGRESS MONITORING

Regular assessments of student's progress toward their IEP goals to ensure that they are making adequate progress and to make any necessary adjustments to their program.

PUNISHMENT

A consequence that decreases the likelihood of a behavior being repeated.

REEVALUATION

An evaluation was conducted for a student with a disability who already receives special education services.

REINFORCEMENT

A consequence that increases the likelihood of a behavior being repeated.

RELATED SERVICES

Related services may be required to assist a student with a disability to receive meaningful educational benefits. These may include counseling, occupational therapy, physical therapy, speech-language therapy, orientation, and mobility services.

REPETITIVE BEHAVIORS

Patterns of behavior that are repeated frequently and appear to serve no purpose.

RESOLUTION MEETING

After a parent's due process complaint is filed, the School District and the parent are provided with an opportunity to meet to discuss possible resolution to the issues of the complaint. This meeting is called a "resolution meeting."

SENSORY INTEGRATION THERAPY
Therapy focuses on improving how an individual processes and responds to sensory information from the environment.

SENSORY PROCESSING DISORDER
A condition where the brain has difficulty processing and interpreting sensory information from the environment.

SERVICES
Special education and related services, such as speech therapy or occupational therapy that a student may receive as part of their IEP.

SHAPING
The process of gradually teaching a new behavior by reinforcing successive to the desired behavior.

SHORT-TERM BENCHMARKS
Short-term objectives are the intermediate steps that must be learned to reach an annual goal. Benchmarks are milestones that the student will demonstrate that lead to an annual goal.

SOCIAL COMMUNICATION
The ability to effectively exchange information with others through speech, nonverbal cues, and other means of communication.

SOCIAL HISTORY
An interview with parents concerning a student's health, family, and school background, including social relationships that are used as part of a student's evaluation.

SOCIAL PRAGMATICS
The social skills needed to effectively communicate and understand social cues in different situations.

SOCIAL SKILLS TRAINING
A type of therapy that focuses on teaching social skills, such as making friends, initiating conversations, and understanding social cues.

SPECIAL CLASS
All students in a special class have IEPs that identify needs that cannot be met in a general education classroom. Special classes are taught by special education teachers, providing specialized instruction.

SPECIALLY DESIGNED INSTRUCTION
Specially designed instruction consists of adaptations to the content, methodology, or delivery of instruction to address the unique needs that result from the child's disability.

SPEECH AND LANGUAGE THERAPY
Therapy focuses on improving communication skills, such as speech production, language comprehension, and social communication.

STIMMING
Self-stimulating behaviors, such as hand-flapping or rocking, are often associated with autism.

THEORY OF MIND
The ability to understand that others have their thoughts, feelings, and beliefs that are different from one's own.

TRANSITION SERVICES
For students with IEPs, "Transition" means planning for life after high school. Beginning when the student is 14, the IEP team will discuss the student's goals, transition needs, and transition activities at each IEP meeting until the student graduates or until the end of the school year in which they turn 21.

VOCATIONAL ASSESSMENT
The Vocational Assessment is used when considering a student's Transition needs, starting during the first IEP in effect during the school year in which the student turns 15.

About the Author

Stephen Cook is a highly acclaimed children's book author and illustrator whose captivating tales have touched the hearts and minds of countless young readers. Stephen's unique journey started as a creative director in the advertising world, His innate ability to tell stories visually laid the foundation for his later endeavors. After years of success in the advertising industry, he embarked on a new path, driven by a profound desire to make a lasting impact on young lives through literature. For the past decade, Stephen has dedicated himself to the fields of training and education, leveraging his creative prowess to develop educational materials that resonate with both educators and students alike.

At the heart of Stephen's passion lies his role as a proud father to an autistic child. This personal journey ignited a fierce dedication to advocating for the special needs community, an advocacy that has spanned over 15 years. Through his writings, Stephen not only educates the public about the challenges faced by individuals with special needs but also provides a beacon of hope and understanding. His commitment to raising awareness and fostering inclusivity is evident in every word he pens.

Stephen's expertise shines in his specialization in educational materials, which includes preparation stories, social narratives, and addressing social-emotional issues. These materials serve as invaluable resources for educators, parents, and caregivers, empowering them to guide children through life's complexities with empathy and resilience. His narratives go beyond the pages, becoming tools for cultivating essential life skills and emotional intelligence.

The core essence of Stephen's work lies in his mission to actively engage young minds in enjoyable and memorable stories. His tales not only entertain but also instill lifelong problem-solving skills, teaching young readers to approach challenges with creativity and confidence. Stephen's inspiration emanates from his close interactions with children and his unwavering commitment to listening to the insights of counselors, parents, and teachers. This commitment ensures that his stories remain attuned to the evolving needs of both the classroom and home environments.

Made in the USA
Coppell, TX
20 January 2024